NORTHUMBERLAND

Stories
of the
Supernatural

Michael J. Hallowell

Foreword by John F. Triplow

COUNTRYSIDE BOOKS
NEWBURY BERKSHIRE

First published 2012
© Michael J. Hallowell 2012

COUNTRYSIDE BOOKS
3 Catherine Road
Newbury, Berkshire

To view our complete range of books,
please visit us at
www.countrysidebooks.co.uk

ISBN 978 1 84674 299 6

For Annie St John
Gone, but not forgotten.

Designed by Peter Davies, Nautilus Design

Produced through MRM Associates Ltd., Reading
Typeset by Mac Style, Beverley, E. Yorkshire
Printed by Berforts Information Press, Oxford

Contents

Acknowledgements

Alan Tedder, for sending me information regarding some wonderful 'ghost ship' tales and other strange Northumbrian stories; Darren W. Ritson for his much-appreciated advice regarding *The Weeping Boy*; Georgina Plowright, curator of the Corbridge Roman Site & Museum, for her advice regarding the mysterious missing legion; Jackie, my wife, for a never-ending supply of tea and patience; John F. Triplow, for his valued input regarding several stories in this book, and for penning the foreword; and the National Coal Mining Museum for England, for advice concerning the story of *Cutty Soames*.

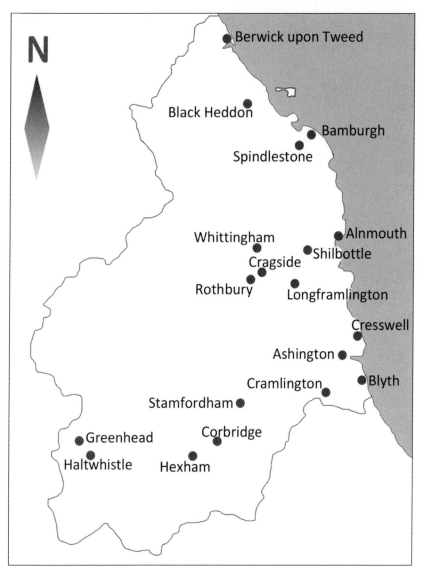

N

Berwick upon Tweed

Black Heddon

Bamburgh

Spindlestone

Whittingham

Alnmouth

Shilbottle

Cragside

Rothbury

Longframlington

Cresswell

Ashington

Cramlington

Blyth

Stamfordham

Corbridge

Greenhead

Haltwhistle

Hexham

Map of Northumberland showing locations of the stories

Foreword

Having been born and bred in Northumberland, it is indeed a true honour to be asked to pen the foreword for this book on the county's spectral inhabitants. It is a subject that has both fascinated and intrigued me since I was a young lad. Over the years I have spent many a night in search of the ghosts, monsters and other denizens of the fourth dimension that haunt the rural areas of this beautiful and enigmatic part of the world.

I remember when I first got to know Mike. I'd read one of his books and, on a whim, decided to drop him a line and tell him how much I'd enjoyed it. Mike has a way of taking the most mundane of stories and, without exaggerating or distorting them one whit, retelling them in such a way that they take on new life and fascination.

As my friendship with Mike grew, I noticed that he seemed to have little interest in the big paranormal stories – wraiths of the rich and famous, headline-grabbing hauntings or 'classic' tales of the supernatural associated with kings and queens, historical monuments or legendary battles. Mike would get just as excited about a long-forgotten UFO story from the 1950s or a haunted bathroom in Blackpool as he would at a sighting of Mary, Queen of Scots, floating along the battlements of a grandiose castle. His interest in the lesser-known stories is a strength, for he is continually adding new or forgotten material to the UK's library of eerie tales.

Whether you choose to believe in preternatural occurrences or not, that's up to you, but an unbiased examination of the facts shows they really do happen. All I ask is that you read through the pages of this book with an open mind, for – you never know – one day you might just end up having such an encounter yourself.

So, without further ado, I will hand you over to my dear friend and colleague Mike Hallowell. He has amassed a fine collection of tales for this volume and I'm sure they will be returned to for many years to come. Enjoy …

John F. Triplow
Paranormal investigator

Introduction

Northumberland is a land of magic and, surprising though it may be to some, I'm convinced that its topography has much to do with this. There are parts of the United Kingdom – areas of Cambridgeshire, for example – which are as flat as the proverbial billiard table. Wherever you stand you can see for miles. Nothing is, or can be, hidden. But Northumberland is far, far different. It is rent by valleys, cleaved by dales and decorated with hills. The roads do not so much traverse the landscape as wiggle their way through it. Travellers can never be truly sure just what lies around the next bend, over the next rise or beyond the next hillock. Whatever else we may say about it, Northumberland is a place which automatically lends itself to tales of the supernatural. Before humans first set foot there, it was already possessed by the eerie beauty which still adorns it.

I've had a few paranormal experiences in my life, although not as many as one might imagine, perhaps, considering that I investigate them full-time for a living. Since the age of eleven I've delved into just about any supernatural discipline one can imagine. I've investigated stories of 'graveyard dogs' in Texas, flying saucers in Amsterdam and giant eels in Geneva and, perhaps inevitably, the time came when the urge to write about them became too strong to resist. In 1998 I was asked to pen a column for my local newspaper, the *Shields Gazette*. WraithScape started out as a weekly dip into the world of paranormal phenomena, and in it I'd write up the experiences of readers who'd contacted me about their own chilling encounters. The column was supposed to last for eight weeks – little more than a series of features, really – but it seemed to captivate the imagination of readers to such an extent that its life was extended. Fourteen years later, and it's still going strong. The stories never stop coming in and my delight at writing them up never ends. Many of those tales have their origin in Northumberland.

There's a misconception that the vast majority of preternatural occurrences in any given location will be ghost stories. Many of them will be, of course, but not necessarily the majority. I happen to be the Tyneside Representative of the Centre for Fortean Zoology – the UK's (and probably the world's) only full-time organisation dedicated to travelling the world in search of real, live monsters. If you think that the nearest thing you'll find to a mystery animal in this neck of the woods is the Loch Ness Monster, you'd be wrong. Northumberland has literally dozens of legends concerning dragons, ape-like creatures and other weird fauna stretching back over the centuries. Investigating them can be an amazing experience.

Ill health has curtailed my 'on-site' investigations somewhat, although not entirely. I've always been a bit of a minimalist when it comes to going on investigations, and usually carry with me nothing more than a good camera and a digital sound recorder. Some investigators carry boxes and bags full of hi-tech equipment with them, but not me. I prefer to travel light, particularly if it's in the heart of rural Northumberland where, depending on the kind of phenomenon I'm investigating, a quick getaway might prove to be a distinct advantage!

And so, on both a professional and a personal level, I have been and continue to be haunted by that ancient, enigmatic place known as Northumberland. In this volume I present some of the strangest tales to come forth from that region. Some are already 'in the public domain', so to speak, and concern supernatural events that have taken place at specific locations in Northumberland. Others are bizarre experiences related to me by Northumbrians during four decades of research. Make of them what you will, but do not imagine they are all flights of fancy. Northumberland is the quintessential supernatural kingdom, the home of things unseen but often sensed. Or, on another day, most certainly seen but little understood.

Each mystery – each enigma, puzzle or miracle – in its own way bids you welcome. All you need do to cross the threshold and enter is to turn the page …

Michael J. Hallowell

The Black Heddon Wraiths

Wraiths are said to be apparitions of those who are about to die; or, if you like, those who have just died. But then again, depending on what sources you trust, a wraith may be simply any old spectre who has taken the trouble to visit you and warn you of an impending death, or of a recent one. In fact, in parts of Northumberland, wraiths were believed to visit people to help them *avoid* dying, not encourage them to shuffle off this mortal coil.

Our tale begins in the Northumberland village of Black Heddon, a name with a certain ring to it which lends itself to eerie stories. A poor woman – some say a widow – lived there, whose impoverished circumstances encouraged her to be creative. Dandelion greens would be added to salads, sailcloth remnants sewn into blankets and fish bones employed as hair combs, that sort of thing. One way in which the woman – by tradition named Esther Morton – saved a few pence was to collect her own firewood. Mind you, most people did that back then. One day, she decided to get up early and look for wood in the field of a nearby farmer. Stick by stick and twig by twig she slowly filled her sack. And then it happened.

Esther bent down to pick up a particularly sturdy branch and, as she stood up, she was mortified to find herself standing face-to-face with the farmer himself. Panicking and perhaps expecting him to yell something like, 'What are you doing with my sticks?', Esther Morton turned tail and fled home.

As she fled, however, she remembered something. The farmer had been really ill in recent days; bedridden, in fact. What was he doing out in the fields? She bumped into a neighbour, related her experience and asked about the farmer.

'Oh, haven't you heard? He's just died …'

Esther Morton had seen the apparition of the farmer at the time he passed away. To some, the spectre would be called a 'crisis apparition', to others it would have been his wraith. Whatever one calls it, it certainly chilled the bones of that poor woman picking firewood.

Now the strange thing about this tale is that it is certainly not the only wraith-related event to take place in Black Heddon. There are others, one of the most fascinating being that of the Strawhouse Wraith.

At around the same time period, although we can't be certain exactly when, William Henderson in his 1866 book, *Folklore of the Northern Counties of England & the Borders*, relates that a farm-hand by the name of William Elliott had a similar experience. Looking out of his window one morning, Elliott saw a neighbour by the name of Mary Brown walking across the fold-yard. This surprised him somewhat, for he knew that Mary had been ill for quite some time. As large as life, she entered the strawhouse, a building used for the storage of straw, as if there was nothing wrong with her.

So ill had Mary been that William realised that there was something intrinsically impossible about what he was seeing. This prompted him to immediately go to the Brown home and enquire about the woman's welfare. He was shocked to be told that Mary had passed away just minutes earlier; at the exact time Elliott had seen her walking across the fold-yard, in fact.

Whatever we may imagine wraiths to be, we have no real reason to doubt the integrity of the Black Heddon residents who claim to have seen them.

The Weeping Boy

There is a universal constant found within the fishing industry. Wherever you may engage in it, it's dangerous. The North Sea, beautiful and awe-inspiring though it is, is not known for its delicate waves and fairy-like froth. It is a tempestuous arm of a violent ocean and has taken untold thousands of lives over the millennia. It is also very treacherous. Even when it appears to be calm, powerful undercurrents snake beneath the surface. And, when the North Sea erupts, fishermen get down on their knees and pray.

Even in the time of the Roman occupation, sailors would throw coins into the sea as they approached the coast to appease a number of deities which could have some influence over their safe passage into harbour. The Vikings did the same and, over the ages, members of a dragon-based cult even carried out human sacrifices. Whatever one's religious perspective, we can all agree that although the North Sea in the 19th century inspired poet and artist alike, it also proved to be a terrible enemy to those who sailed it in ships to access its bounty. Being a Northumbrian fisherman was a hard, hard life.

The following story has its setting during one of the great storms which have wreaked havoc along the English coastline ever since records were kept. I'm convinced it is based on a real event and is not merely an urban myth, so the question is whether we can pinpoint a specific time-period which fits the story as it has been passed down. My research allowed me to narrow it down to two.

The worst storm ever recorded in England was the Great Storm which devastated the south of England on the evening of Monday, 26th November 1703. Some estimates put the number of dead at 15,000, others double that. The difficulty is that only the faintest traces of the storm touched Berwick upon Tweed, and my research has thrown up no deaths there, on land or at sea, which can be attributed to it.

A far more likely candidate is the Great Storm of 1881, at the heart of which was Berwickshire in Scotland. Equally victimized was Berwick upon Tweed in England. During the storm, 196 fishermen lost their lives. Most were from Eyemouth, but some were from other towns and villages. To this day, the event is known as Black Friday.

The legend is that for some days before the storm a young boy of Berwick had felt a growing sense of unease about his father and brothers who were about to go on a fishing trip in the family's boat. When it was pointed out to him, in an effort to assuage his fears, that they had always returned home safely before and there was no reason why this time should be any different, it did nothing to pacify him.

The Great Storm struck, of course, and the family faced a knotty problem: to sail or not to sail. Bad though the weather was, there seems to have been a general consensus that it was not bad enough to prevent the trip going ahead. And so it was that the father and two of his sons pulled out of the harbour on the River Tweed, leaving behind them an extremely disturbed young man.

When the time approached for the boat to return, the young lad decided to go down and meet it, even though, deep down inside, he harboured an awful feeling that it would not return at all. Nothing his mother and sisters said had pacified him. Outside the weather was grim; the rain fell in torrents, the wind blew at gale force and thunder peals rent the cloud-laden skies. Regardless, he slipped out of the cottage and made his way to the dock. The boat did not return, and, as darkness fell, he made his way home. The following day, at dawn, he once more made his way to the dock. The storm had not abated; in fact it had grown worse. Again the boat failed to return, and now even the boy's mother and sisters were becoming disturbed.

On the third day the boy once again made his lonely vigil, and had now convinced himself that his father and brothers were dead. As the rain whipped about him he sunk to his knees and began sobbing. It is said that his anguished cries could be heard over quite a distance, eventually prompting one local woman to walk down to the dock and investigate. There she found the distraught youngster, whom she helped to his feet and then took him home. The family's fishing boat never returned from that fateful trip.

Now there are a number of strange aspects to this story which need addressing. The shade of the young man has often been seen and heard, and it is said that his appearance always precedes either a death or disaster. This is not an unknown phenomenon in the world of paranormal research, but the truly odd thing is that it is apparently the ghost of the young boy which appears, even though he did not die in the storm, and not the spectres of the fishermen who did perish. An unusually large number of ghosts are those of people who have died sudden or violent deaths, but not all fit into this category. As far as I have been able to determine, the young man did not die a premature or violent death, so why does his ghost – if that is what it truly is – appear as a young child?

It may be that the apparition of the young man is not a ghost at all in the true sense of the word, but simply what some researchers call an 'imprint', a visual vignette of an intensely emotional moment caught in time. It is as if the environment somehow captures moments like these – how we don't know – and can 'replay' them. As far as I am aware there is no scientific proof to support the theory, but there is much anecdotal evidence which points in that direction.

The setting of the tale is also open to some debate. In some versions the story is dislocated from any particular town or village, and is simply set 'somewhere on the Northumberland coast'. Darren W. Ritson, who is arguably the leading living expert on Northumbrian ghost lore, places the story in Berwick and I'm pretty sure he's correct.

The one puzzle that remains is that I can find no records detailing the deaths of the three fishermen during 1881. Although the keeping of parish records was not as meticulous back then as we sometimes imagine, it is inconceivable that three deaths in such tragic circumstances would have gone unrecorded. Also, there seems to be no record in the contemporary media of the tragedy. One explanation is that the event did not take place in Berwick at all, but somewhere else in Northumberland. However, my instinct is that it probably did take place in Berwick though perhaps much earlier than 1881.

In any event, the story is deeply moving. The image of a small laddie, sobbing on a windswept dock awaiting in vain the return of his family, is not an easy one to forget.

3

The Schooner Hotel

Alnmouth is one of the quaintest places one could hope to visit. It flaunts architectural styles ancient and modern, and all of them are married in a way that pleases the senses. Unfortunately, the aura of tranquillity it exudes now masks a long and, at times, turbulent history, much of it rooted in supernatural phenomena. It has been invaded by the Scots, devastated by the Black Death and touched by more than a few murders.

But it wasn't all bad. Alnmouth developed an unrivalled reputation as a trading port, and the fishermen had an expertise that equalled any on the north-east coast. Like other coastal villages, it provided typical entertainment for its residents in the form of alcohol and tobacco so it wasn't long before a hostelry sprung up where they could enjoy both. Its name was the Schooner Inn. As well as selling liquor, it also offered lodgings to travellers and, after a while, became home to several ghosts.

Externally, the Schooner exemplifies everything one expects from a quaint village pub: a smart black-and-white frontage, mock shutters and a colourful sign which sways gently in the breeze. But inside it harbours secrets, such as a tunnel which runs from the cellar to the coast and that, at one time, was used by smugglers, press gangs and wanted criminals alike.

One of the most intriguing and brutal tales to come out of the Schooner concerns a French family – mother, father and two children – who arrived to stay at the inn. Theories as to just why a Gallic family of good reputation would end up staying at the

Schooner vary. Some say they had relatives in the town – not impossible – but the repeated fisticuffs between the English and our friends on the Continent during the 17th century, when this incident was said to have taken place, do make their arrival rather odd to say the least.

As the family made their way upstairs to their room, they were followed by a thief who, it is alleged, knocked them all unconscious. He then dragged them into Room 28 and slit their throats before making off with their valuables. Or so the story goes.

Another version is that the French father himself killed the other members before committing suicide. Why he'd travel from France to Alnmouth to do this, though, is a conundrum of the first order. In fact, whichever version of the tale suits you, there isn't a shred of evidence that the incident ever occurred – or that the family even existed. Mind you, that's not to say it didn't happen, for there's an old maxim that 'absence of evidence is not evidence of absence'.

My colleague John Triplow happened to be present in Room 28 at the Schooner on one occasion, when a medium, in the adjacent hallway, stated that the spirit of a French male by the name of Max was present in the room. Max apparently became highly indignant if any females addressed him by his first name, preferring instead to be called Papa. This all fits nicely with the story of the French family who allegedly died in that room centuries earlier.

John and another fellow pensmith, Darren Ritson have both carried out intensive investigations at the Schooner. Intriguingly, a number of guests at the inn claim to have been grabbed around the neck as if an invisible pair of hands was trying to throttle them. Even more curious, all of these incidents seem to have taken place in Room 4.

When John Triplow attended the Schooner in August of 2009, he certainly came away with food for thought. A female guest suddenly found dusty handprints on her thighs, although she had no idea how they got there. But there was more. Researcher and photographer Gail Ward was standing on the bottom step of the flight leading into the cellar when, suddenly, one of the younger guests jumped up from his seat and raced for the exit. Gail, who witnessed the incident, said it was pretty obvious the lad was genuinely scared of something. Later, when interviewed, the witness repeatedly broke down in tears. Another was grabbed around the ankle and fled. Yet another saw a dark figure crouching in an even darker corner.

A colleague of John Triplow's who had also spent time at the Schooner told him,

'You know, I had a really creepy experience there a few years back. I was on a ghost tour with some friends and we had gathered in Room 5 with several other guests. What I saw will stay with me for the rest of my life. We were sitting in the dark when suddenly I noticed a little girl standing in the room. What disturbed me most of all was the fact that she was on fire. I wasn't the only one that could see her either. The experience was so intense I could feel the heat and actually taste the smoke … It was horrible. I just had to leave the room.'

The Schooner still stands, and its ghosts still seem to walk its corridors.

4

My Grandfather's Watch

Some years ago I received a letter from Christine Winters of Cleadon village, who told me about a strange experience she'd had when her father died. A reporter from my local paper and I went to interview her. The reporter lost interest – quite understandably – when she discovered that the incident in question hadn't occurred in South Tyneside itself, but in Ashington. For the reporter it had lost its local flavour; for me, it had suddenly sprouted wings.

'It was 1978, and I was living in Ashington at the time', she said, 'and Grandpa John was in the terminal stages of lung cancer'. At exactly 8.08 pm, Grandpa John had taken a deep breath and slumped back on his pillow, leaving behind a grieving widow, four children and seven grandchildren. Later, his eldest daughter Maureen removed his wristwatch and noticed that it had stopped ticking. The hands had stopped moving at the exact moment he had passed away. She showed it to Christine, who was stunned.

This isn't the first tale I've heard of this nature. There have been many occasions when clocks and watches have stopped working at the very time when their owners have shuffled off this mortal coil. To be honest, I haven't a clue why this happens. But it does.

In 1876, the celebrated American composer Henry Clay Work published a song that became a classic, *My Grandfather's Clock*. The song told the tale of an old man whose clock stopped on the day that he died and it has become the theme tune for those who have witnessed clocks and watches stop at the exact time a relative has passed away. One theory is that people can form such a close attachment to personal possessions that when they pass over, the artefacts almost lose the will to 'live' themselves and no longer function.

Scientifically speaking, of course, there isn't a shred of proof that such a thing can happen. Yet, there are many instances on record that provide good circumstantial evidence that something odd is indeed taking place.

In 1972, Middlesbrough woman Evelyn Sibbey reported how a grandfather clock that had been in her family since 1912 had mysteriously stopped working seven times. On each occasion a close family member had just died.

In 1983 an antique dealer from Walsall in the West Midlands purchased a large clock which was in perfect working order. Four days later the clock stopped, and no matter what the new owner did he could not get it to start again. Later he discovered that the chap who had sold it to him had died of a heart attack at the time that the clock had 'expired'.

Perhaps the strangest tale is that of a grandfather clock which stopped working in 1947 when its owner, a London docker called John Thompson, died of pneumonia. The clock stood in his family's hallway for several years afterwards, but stubbornly refused to work. That is, until one of John's daughters gave birth to a child. At the precise time his granddaughter came into the world, the clock started ticking again.

The mysterious case of the grandfather's watch which stopped working in Ashington, then, is certainly not unique. However, there is a very strange postscript to this tale for I was subsequently contacted by Christine Winter's sister, Maureen. I was deeply sorry to hear that Christine had passed away. Like her father, she'd succumbed to lung cancer. 'I was with Christine when she died', Maureen said. 'I held her hand and waited till she passed away. It was just after 7.30 pm.'

Two days after Christine's funeral, their youngest sister, Kimber, was walking to a local Chinese take-away in Ashington. As she turned the corner she noticed something lying on the ground – a wristwatch. She picked it up and thought it looked suspiciously like the one their grandfather had once owned. Now, she knew that her sister, Maureen had pawned their grandfather's watch some time ago when she had come upon hard times. Kimber took it home and when Maureen saw it, she confirmed immediately that it was indeed their grandfather's watch.

Of course, I assumed that the point to the story was the incredible coincidence that had taken place, that is, Kimber finding their grandfather's watch in the street. The family had been startled by this, of course – it was pretty amazing – but something even more amazing was that an aunt at the house noticed that the hands on the watch pointed to 7.32 – the exact time that Christine had died.

Maureen said she could not help but wonder at what time the hands would be pointing the next time someone in the family died. I wondered too, but we shall never know, for I was later told that Kimber had buried the watch near a churchyard at Ashington.

5

The Hand of Glory

On first hearing, this story sounds like the product of a truly fevered imagination. It involves a daring thief disguised as an elderly widow who, one stormy night, hoodwinks his way into a rural hostelry. Once inside, he does something which by any standards is bizarre. From a bag he removes a wizened, severed hand, the fingertips of which he sets alight with a taper. The fingertips crackle, spit and burn, and give off a peculiar, pungent aroma. As it drifts around the inn, it is inhaled by the sleeping lodgers and members of the household, all of whom then fall into a far, far deeper state of slumber. Once this is accomplished, the thief then lets in several accomplices who have been waiting outside and they promptly begin to avail themselves of anything valuable.

A crazy story, of that there can be no doubt – correct? Actually, the story is, to those who know the facts, entirely plausible.

From the mid 15th century onwards, a rather strange notion spread through Europe and beyond. It was commonly called the Legend of the Hand of Glory. Versions of it were passed on from generation to generation throughout what are now known as the British Isles, and also northern Europe, Scandinavia, South America and remote parts of Russia. Quite simply, the notion was that the left or 'sinister' hand of a hanged man, otherwise known as the Hand of Glory, had the bizarre ability to send people into a coma-like sleep if its fingertips were lit. But simply lighting the fingers was not enough. First, the hand had to be put through a complex process of preparation, the method of which was known to only a few. The most important part of the procedure was to steep the dried hand in an elixir made to a precise formula, but which included beeswax, oil of sesame, vervain and essence of mandrake. Indeed, it is here where we gain our first clue which will help us solve the mystery. The herb mandrake derives its name from the French *maindeglorie*, which means 'hand of glory'. Now it just so happens that mandrake, along with vervain, has powerful sleep-inducing properties and both herbs can, if ingested in sufficient quantities, allegedly render one unconscious. Perhaps, then, there maybe some scientific rationale behind the idea that inhaling fumes from these two plants could send one into a state of deep slumber. Having set the scene, we can now proceed to our story.

In the 18th century, the Old Spital was a welcoming inn situated between the picturesque towns of Brough and Barnard Castle. Late one evening, according to legend, during one of the worst winter storms in memory, and not long after the landlord and his family had retired to bed, the cook was alone on the ground floor making the place presentable for business the next day. Suddenly, she heard a loud banging at the door of the inn, which she promptly answered. To her surprise she found herself staring at what appeared to be a frail, elderly woman shivering in the snow-ridden wind. The cook did what any human being with a conscience would have done, of course, and quickly bid her enter before closing the door.

Shivering violently, the elderly lady explained that she was homeless and had nowhere to rest her head for the night. The cook explained that the inn was full, but there was no way she was going to turn her out again into the storm. Therefore, she prepared a makeshift 'shake-me-down' on a bench in the kitchen, bade the old woman goodnight and made for the door. However, just as she was about to enter the hallway, she spotted something which both alarmed and intrigued her; under the old woman's long dress she could see what looked distinctly like a pair of male pantaloons. Leaving the door ever so slightly ajar, she peered through the crack and watched.

Stunned, she watched for some time as the 'elderly lady' – who by now she realised was patently a man – removed from a bag a wizened human hand. The man then produced a small bottle, removed the stopper and dripped a strange liquid to the tip of each finger. He then lit each finger in turn with a taper, but became irritated when the fifth digit refused to ignite.

To understand just what was transpiring here, it is important to grasp one of the finer nuances of Hand of Glory lore; specifically, that if all of the fingers readily ignite, this is indicative of the fact that every single person in the household is asleep. However, each finger that refuses to ignite is indicative of one person on the premises who is currently awake apart from the person performing the ritual. The cook knew this and figured that the thief was now aware that someone – her good self – was still awake. Frightened, she quickly paddled up the stairwell to the landlord's quarters and desperately attempted to wake him. It was in vain. The landlord and his wife, like everyone else in the building were in a trance-like sleep.

Downstairs, the thief had lost no time in opening the door of the inn for his fellow ne'er-do-wells. They were already packing up everything of value they could lay their hands upon. And, unfortunately, the only person in a position to do anything about it was the old cook. Just as well, then, that she had a plan up her sleeve.

According to legend, the only way to break the enchantment of the Hand of Glory was to extinguish the burning digits by throwing a pan of skimmed milk over them. How fortunate it was, then, that there just happened to be a pan of skimmed milk upon the stove. She crept into the kitchen, picked up the milk and, when the opportunity presented itself, poured it over the burning hand. At once the spell was shattered. The landlord, his sons and a number of burly lodgers woke at once and ran downstairs in time to apprehend the robbers. By dawn they had all been taken off to jail, and the hand – as per the custom – was buried beneath the local gibbet.

Whatever we may make of the tale – and parts of it are admittedly hard to swallow – there is no doubt that the Old Spital Inn existed. It was in fact the original name of what is now the Bowes Moor Hotel which stands at the same location in Barnard Castle.

6

The Phantom Car

One of the most prolific correspondents from whom I receive stories is a reader of my newspaper columns who prefers to be known, simply, as Dorothy Thursday. On one occasion, Mrs Thursday related a tale to me in a letter. It was truly baffling, as you will see, but certainly not unique. I've investigated many stories of 'ghost cars' over the years, and I don't recall a single one that didn't set the hairs on the back of my neck on end. I don't know why, but they have an eerie quality different to any other in the annals of paranormal research.

'My friend and I were looking forward to a few days' holiday in the Lake District', said Dorothy. 'We hadn't seen one another for a few months since leaving university and starting our careers in different parts of the country. I was driving and by the time I had picked her up at the railway station in Newcastle it was getting dark. We enjoyed the journey and chatted about our respective jobs. We had just passed Hexham, on our way to Carlisle when it started to rain. It was two or three years since I had driven in that area, so I was particularly careful and concentrated on the road.'

Being unsure of the terrain, and with the rain increasing in intensity, she wasn't going to take any chances. However, as Dorothy related, even if she had been a bit of a daredevil behind the wheel, she wouldn't have been able to drive fast anyway for, in front of her car was another vehicle which was travelling very slowly; slowly, that is, except when Dorothy tried to overtake it.

'I couldn't get up any speed because of the car in front. We had been following it for some time and, on a couple of occasions, I had tried to overtake it, but it just increased in speed. My friend and I agreed that it would be safer to stay behind until we came to the dual carriageway. The road was quiet, probably because most people had arrived at their destinations and were settling down to dinner. We were excited about visiting mutual friends in the Lakes, and wondered what time we would arrive.'

But then something strange happened. The vehicle in front which was beginning to irritate the two friends suddenly disappeared.

'I looked at my friend and almost simultaneously we both exclaimed, "What happened to the car?" As far as we could recollect there had been no exit to the left or right, and the car had not flashed its indicator. One minute it was in front and the next we were on our own.'

It's natural in cases like this for witnesses to start searching for rational explanations. Seeing something like that – something that just doesn't make sense – has a way of unsettling folk. It also gives the lie to sceptics who argue that people who claim to have undergone supernatural experiences are simply fantasy-prone 'believers', desperately wanting to think that there's more to this world than we can see. Dorothy Thursday and her friend did not want to believe that the car in front of them had simply vanished into the ether before their very eyes.

'The more we talked about it, the more we needed to set our minds to rest. At the next exit I turned the car around and drove back the way we had come. We kept our eyes glued to the sides of the road and I drove as slowly as I dared, even though there was hardly any traffic. We travelled for a few miles and could find no sign of another road or even a farm track. Eventually we decided that something strange had happened but we could not come to a conclusion regarding exactly what.'

In short, there was simply nowhere that the car could have gone without breaking the laws of physics.

'To this day we still talk about the incident', she told me, 'and wonder about the mystery of the disappearing car. Both of us are very sceptical, and have never experienced anything paranormal. However, there is one thing we do know – the car disappeared in front of our very eyes.'

In her correspondence Dorothy asked me a question, 'For the record, there was another event that night in the Carlisle area. We heard later, on the news, that there had been a minor earth tremor. Was this just a coincidence or could the two events be related?'

We'll return to that question presently, but first let me say this: one of the things which impressed me about the encounter was that both women in the car became startled at exactly the same moment in time when the car in front vanished from sight. Let us imagine that the vehicle had, hypothetically speaking, turned off onto a side road even though the friends both testified that no such turning existed. Had the car turned off the road, the driver would surely have indicated left or right. One would have thought that at least one of the witnesses would have seen an indicator light flashing. An even greater likelihood is that the two women would have seen the car itself turn off. I asked Dorothy if it was possible the poor weather conditions could have reduced their visibility just enough so that they didn't see the vehicle ahead turn off the road, but she denied this adamantly.

'True, it was raining, but it wasn't a torrential downpour or anything like that. We could see ahead pretty well … and in any case there just wasn't anywhere the car could have turned.'

But what about the minor earth tremor? Could Dorothy be right? Is it possible that, unlikely though it seems, the two events could be connected? There is a theory that earthquakes can precipitate discharges of electrical energy; discharges so severe that they can affect the human brain and can make witnesses hallucinate. It has been argued that those affected in this way may see strange lights and apparitions, smell weird odours and experience bizarre physiological and psychological symptoms which make them disoriented. It's a fascinating thought but, alas, it doesn't fly. The difficulty is that even if they had experienced some sort of physiological reaction to the earth tremor, why would they have both 'imagined' seeing exactly the same thing: a motor vehicle on the road ahead of them which, they both stated, categorically disappeared at exactly the same moment in time?

There just doesn't seem to be a reasonably plausible explanation for what these two friends witnessed. All we can say is that they saw a motor vehicle disappear right in front of their eyes, and they're unlikely ever to forget it.

7

The Ghostly Legionaries

Some years ago, a former colleague of mine told me of a strange experience he'd had whilst walking near the Arbeia Roman Fort in South Shields.

One Sunday morning, whilst walking down Fort Street, he turned and looked through the iron railings which fence Arbeia off from the pavement. Suddenly, he had an overpowering feeling that he was being watched. Strangely, he seemed to know where the person who was watching him was standing – in amongst the ruins – and yet there was no one there.

Other people who have visited ancient sites also report such feelings, and sometimes they may actually find themselves transported through time and able to witness events which occurred hundreds or even thousands of years ago. The Treasury House in York, for example, is famous for producing a 'time slip' involving Roman soldiers who were once stationed there. Engineer Harry Martindale had one of the most terrifying encounters of all there. Whilst working on his own in the cellar of the Treasury House, Harry was astonished to hear a trumpet call. Then, to his amazement, a solid figure in Roman military dress 'walked out of the wall' in front of him. The apparition was that of a soldier wearing a tunic and carrying a round shield. Terrified, Harry ran to the corner of the cellar and cowered down, watching in astonishment as the first figure was then followed by an officer on horseback and a procession of legionaries.

As this procession walked through the cellar, Harry noticed that they were only visible from the thigh upwards. It was as if the legionaries were walking on a surface at least two feet below the current level of the cellar floor. Martindale later speculated that they were walking on the surface of an old Roman road directly underneath the Treasury House, and it is now known that such a road did indeed exist. Intriguingly, sceptics poured scorn on Harry's story, arguing that Roman legionaries did not carry circular shields. However, at least one legion stationed at York – the VI Victrix – was supported by auxiliary units; and these auxiliaries carried circular or oval shields!

The Roman garrison stationed at Corbridge, Northumberland, was made up of cohorts seconded from a number of the legions garrisoned in Britain. The first to be stationed at Corbridge, called *Corstopitum* by the Romans, was the Legio II Augusta which had formerly been stationed at Caerleon in South Wales. Later, they were relieved by cohorts of the Legio VI Victrix which were relocated from York. In subsequent times, various and sundry units of soldiers from other legions were also stationed there. Eventually, of course, as the whole world knows, the Roman Empire collapsed and the Romans withdrew from Britain. Corbridge then entered into a painfully slow decline, becoming the ruin that historians and tourists alike marvel over today.

Ghosts are traditionally believed to have a shelf-life of sorts; slowly fading away until, after three or four hundred years at most, they are at best noticeable by a vague and momentary 'sense of presence'. For some reason, however, ghosts from the time of the Roman occupation of Britain seem to last much longer. They are seen today, often in full colour and appearing completely solid, so much so that some witnesses report that they initially thought they were looking at actors in an outdoor pageant of some kind.

Radio presenter Alan Robson in his book *Grisly Trails and Ghostly Tales* details a wonderful account, if it is true, concerning the mysterious disappearance of a Roman Legion near Corbridge. I've heard vague rumours of this event from other sources, but whether those who repeated them drew their story from Robson's book, or whether Robson himself heard the tales and then wrote them up, I cannot say.

The gist of the story is that in the year AD 126, the Fifth Legion visited Corstopitum to replenish their rations and assist local craftsmen in the repair of an aqueduct. According to Robson, after their work was done the legionaries left Corstopitum by marching through the Portgate. They then proceeded along the path known as the Devil's Causeway in the direction of Hartburn. This makes good sense from a historical perspective. However, it is what happened next that attaches a real degree of mystery to the tale. According to legend, the soldiers simply disappeared. Robson states, 'It is believed that they either ran away … or were attacked and killed'. Robson admits that the former of the two options is highly unlikely given the disciplined nature of the Roman army.

This story presents us with a problem, however, because Britain was never visited by the Fifth Legion at all, which is a devastating blow to this otherwise intriguing tale. But there is another problem. The aqueduct at Corstopitum, the remains of which can be seen today, *didn't exist* in the year AD 126. If there was a prior aqueduct there, there is no evidence of it. However, on the positive side, there is some evidence that a fire may have taken place around the year AD 125, so the notion that a detachment of soldiers could have been sent to help with the repair work is feasible. If this happened, and we really have no evidence of it, one thing we know for certain is that it wasn't the Fifth Legion.

We do know that, in the year AD 117, the Ninth Legion (*Legio IX Hispana)*, marched north into Scotland and did indeed disappear in mysterious circumstances. This, though, was a full eight years before the alleged disappearance of Robson's Fifth Legion in AD 125. In any event, although the almost unanimous opinion of scholars used to be that the Ninth must have been massacred and their remains quickly buried, it is now generally thought that the legion was simply transferred abroad. Indeed, there is some historical evidence for this.

Altogether then, some aspects of the tale as presented by Robson are completely untenable, whilst others are not unreasonable. All we can say is that the essence of the story he presents is possible, but that it could not have happened in the historical context he offers.

Certainly, some individuals do claim to have seen legionaries in that vicinity, for I've interviewed two of them myself.

The first was an eldery chap who was inspecting the Roman ruins at Corbridge circa 1998 – when 'a sudden wind whipped up'. Albert Allen, a retired bus driver, turned and was certain that, for the briefest of moments, he saw a soldier holding a spear and an oval shield standing near one of the foundations. The oval shield would indicate that the legionary was an auxiliary. Albert was able to provide few other details, but did add that the figure appeared to be wearing a helmet of some sort. No sooner had he spotted it, though, than it disappeared.

The second witness, who does not wish to be named, also claimed to have seen a solitary legionary sitting on the remains of a wall. The problem with this is that the wall would not have been a low ruin back then, so the question arises as to how a spectre from hundreds of years ago can sit upon a wall as it is now, and not as it would have been during his life 'in the flesh', so to speak. Intriguingly, this conundrum is not uncommon in ghost sightings, and I have come across a number of such anomalies. In one, the ghost of a Cavalier would often be seen sitting on a stool at a bar which did not even exist in the ancient pub during that era. Puzzling though it is, I'm reluctant to dismiss such cases simply because there's an aspect to them that we don't yet understand. I think the real answer lies in the nature of ghosts which, although they are very real, are not I would venture the 'spirits of the dead', but something stranger altogether.

Whatever the truth of the tale, the apparitions of Roman legionaries do seem to haunt Corbridge. As for the lost legion, I know of no more mystical image than that of a ghostly troupe of Roman soldiers silently walking into the mist, and then oblivion. If the story isn't true, it's so wonderful it should be.

8

The Villages Lost in Time

Some time ago, whilst shopping in Newcastle's Chinatown, a reader of one of my columns espied my wife and gingerly approached. After introducing herself, she said that she'd been meaning to write in for some time with a question, but had always ended up binning her efforts halfway through on the basis that I might have thought she was silly. I'm not sure why, as her question was a perfectly sensible one.

I asked the reader, beauty therapist Edie Bouchard, just what her question was.

'To tell the truth, I used to think that time was sort of in a line … you know, past, present and future. But then I read about a woman who said that she'd got lost in Berlin one day, turned a corner and ended up in the year 1917. She claimed she'd gone back through time. I know it sounds daft, but I keep worrying that the same thing could happen to me. It's become an obsession, really.'

Now, just because time travel isn't possible as far as we know, that doesn't mean that people can't glimpse the past, which is an entirely different thing. The truth is that looking into the past is as easy as falling off a log, costs no money and you can, if you wish, do it this very night. Sceptical?

Open your door after dark and look up into the night sky. You'll see an uncountable number of stars. Each one of those stars is light years away from planet earth. Some are only five or six light years away, others hundreds. When we look at a star which is, say, twenty light years away, we're seeing it not as it is now, but as it was twenty years ago as it's taken the light twenty years to reach us. Just by looking at that one star, we're literally looking back twenty years into the past. Therefore, it becomes self-evident that when we stare at dozens of stars we are actually looking back through the years at many different time periods at once.

Several years ago I interviewed a couple who had visited Northumberland two summers previously. They'd booked into a B&B in Alnwick and spent a lazy few days meandering around our breathtaking countryside. Lunches were taken in picturesque pubs and afternoons spent exploring castles and stately homes; they couldn't have been happier. One day, after picking up several bits and pieces at a car boot sale, they decided to head back to their digs before visiting a nearby pub for a nightcap. On the way, they happened to spot a cottage at the side of the road. It wasn't in the best condition – it was somewhat ramshackle, to be honest – but they both agreed it possessed a large degree of charm. Linda Williams told me it reminded her of the sort of thing one would find featuring in a Catherine Cookson novel. Her husband, Boris, agreed, 'It really was enchanting ... it was "picture postcard perfect" as they say'. Linda, who was driving, pulled into a makeshift lay-by on the other side of the road and retrieved her camera from the back seat of the car. She stepped out and quickly took two pictures of the cottage, slightly apprehensive that someone might see her and wonder what on earth she was up to. The couple then resumed their journey.

Two or three days passed by and, after another busy morning motoring, Linda and Boris found themselves driving not too far away from the cottage that had enchanted them so much. They decided to make a slight detour and take another look. To their surprise, they didn't find the cottage when they turned the corner – instead they were confronted by something altogether different – a working post office. It was quaint, picturesque, but of a distinctly more modern provenance. Naturally, they assumed they'd taken a wrong turning but then Linda spotted something. Across the road from the post office was the lay-by they'd parked in several days earlier.

'There was no doubt in my mind it was the same lay-by', said Linda. 'There was a litter bin on a wooden post – I remembered that – and a large boulder painted white. Boris was convinced there had to be a rational explanation, and so was I.'

The couple stood talking for a while, but simply couldn't come up with an answer that made any sense. Finally, they decided to pop into the post office to see if anyone inside could shed some light on the matter. The postmaster wasn't in, but an elderly woman was serving behind the shop counter. She said she couldn't be sure, but she believed that there used to be a cottage on the site where the post office now stood. She didn't know when it had been demolished, and as it had already disappeared from the landscape when she was a child she had no recollection of what it had looked like. Linda and Boris eventually returned home, and one of the first things they did was to get their photographs developed.

'I honestly didn't think the picture of the cottage would come out', said Boris. 'I just had this feeling that it would be blank, or something, and we wouldn't have any proof we'd seen it.' But the picture did 'come out'. It wasn't perfect; the colours were faded almost to the point where it appeared to be monochrome, and the right-hand side was faded to white. Still, the cottage could be seen clearly, exactly as they'd remembered it.

When I first covered the story, I was interested to see whether there were any background features – hills, mounds, roadways – that could positively identify the location as being exactly the same as the one where the post office now stood. Sadly, there weren't. I wanted to visit myself and talk to the postmaster, but Linda didn't feel comfortable about that. They'd telephoned the postmaster, she said, and hadn't received an enthusiastic response. 'He didn't want his business labelled as a haunted building', she told me, 'and was really concerned that the newspapers would start making a song and dance about it. We talked about it and decided not to take it any further; we didn't want such an incredible story to end on a sour note. We still have our picture, and that's enough, I suppose.'

The couple did make one or two further enquiries – discreet ones – and managed to establish that the cottage on the site had been demolished in 1926. As for Edie Bouchard, there wasn't much I could say to comfort her, except that the number of people who claim to have experienced time travel are very few indeed.

The strange experience related to me by Linda and Boris Williams wasn't the only one of its kind to take place in Northumberland, though. In 1946, Linda Craig from Liverpool came on a visit with her grandparents for a week's holiday. It wasn't long before she became bored with the country cottage they were staying in and decided to do 'some exploring' as she put it.

Linda couldn't remember the name of the village where she stayed, but she did recall that there were three shops there: a general dealer's, a post office and a small dairy outlet next to a nearby farm. Curious, she visited each shop in turn. She didn't purchase anything, she just looked at the goods on the shelves and then moved on. She'd particularly liked the shop attached to the dairy and recalled talking at length with the elderly woman behind the counter. 'She gave me a glass of milk, the best I'd ever tasted', she said.

The following day Linda walked along the lane again, fully intending to visit the dairy a second time in the hope of getting yet another glass of milk, but couldn't find it. The dairy, along with the adjacent shop, was nowhere to be seen. Puzzled, she returned to the holiday cottage and asked her grandmother where the dairy shop was. Her grandmother, also puzzled, told her that the old dairy had been demolished during the First World War.

I discussed the case with a colleague, and we both realised that the grandmother must have had some sort of connection with the village; otherwise, how could she have known the fate of the old dairy all those years ago? We weren't sure what sort of influence this might have had on Linda's experience, if any, unless one accepts the controversial theory of genetically inherited memory. Had Linda recalled something which her grandmother had actually experienced decades earlier? We can but guess. Had she travelled back in time? It's tempting to believe so, but too much water has passed under the temporal bridge now. All we can do is marvel at a truly mysterious tale.

9

The Phantom Hunt

Haltwhistle, despite not being the largest conurbation on God's earth, certainly plays host to a fair number of spectres. One of the most chilling is that of the Phantom Hunt, which consists not of one ghost but dozens: horses, men, hounds and a solitary fox.

Peter Underwood, who has recorded the story in his book, *The A-Z of British Ghosts*, spends little time spelling out the detail of the haunting but makes the point that when the phantom hunt is seen, it has the most disturbing effect on animals in the vicinity. Cats, dogs and birds are driven into a state of frenzy by the approach of the oldest – or at least the scariest – hunt in existence.

The question arises – just what kind of hunt are we talking about here? The phantom echo of red-jacketed fox-hunters in the style of John Peel? Or something even older?

There is a common misconception that 'the Hunt' is a relatively modern idea, stretching back no further than, say, the 16th century. In fact, it is an activity which goes back to the earliest days of human civilisation. It was extremely popular with the Romans, and I have a 2nd-century drinking vessel with a hunting scene delicately embossed around its circumference. Other than the absence of traditional English headgear, there is little difference between the Roman hunt on the pot and that engaged in by enthusiasts in the 21st century. There is nothing new under the sun, as the saying goes.

It may not be coincidence, then, that the Phantom Hunt of Haltwhistle is seen most often close to the remains of the Roman Wall nearby.

In 2004, a fellow columnist Anna Kaye and I gave a lecture in Alnwick to a group of people enthusiastic about the supernatural. At least 50% of the audience openly admitted to having had their own ghost sighting, or at least an 'eerie experience' of some kind. One man admitted to having both seen – and heard – the Phantom Hunt of Haltwhistle. His story, which I can unfortunately only paraphrase as best as my memory allows, was as follows:

'I was walking along a stretch of Hadrian's Wall early one summer's evening and, being a bit of a twitcher, I was enjoying the last of the bird-song. I've always found it immensely peaceful walking along the Wall. On this occasion, however, I noticed something very strange. The birds suddenly went completely silent; you couldn't hear a single one of them. I started to feel a bit uncomfortable to be honest, and I was thinking about turning back when I heard the sound of men shouting in the distance. I'm not sure what it was, but even though I couldn't make out what they were shouting there was something odd about their voices; they sounded a bit foreign.

'Not long after I heard the voices, I also heard the sound of horses' hooves thumping on the ground. They were getting louder very quickly and I remember taking a good few steps backwards and standing behind some stones as I didn't want to get trampled on. I also heard dogs baying.

'What I saw was so strange I can hardly describe it. To my left I could see something approaching in the distance. Roughly it looked like two horses side-by-side, but the colours were all blurred. It was like seeing blurred photographs, only in motion. As everything got closer, the ground was shaking with the sound of the horses and there was barking, shouting … it was chaos. But all I could see was a jumble of colour, shape and shadow whizzing past. Then everything went quiet. The sounds faded away, the weird shapes disappeared and everything returned to normal. To this day I don't know what happened. I still go back up there, but just not to that particular stretch.'

Just what this chap saw baffled Anna and me, but I think there's enough circumstantial evidence to suggest it was the Phantom Hunt of Haltwhistle, and that it may have been an ancient Roman hunt and not a collection of our red-coated English riders out enjoying themselves. Still, I'm open to reason…

10

Nellie the Knocker

Tales of phantoms directing people to the sites of buried treasure are common – a veritable cluster of them have their home in South Shields, not far south of Northumberland – but one of the strangest has to be that of the Grey Lady of Haltwhistle. (For the record, phantoms in the shape of grey ladies are incredibly common too, but not like this one.)

Our story begins at a farm not far from Haltwhistle where, allegedly, a stone of monumental proportions sat nearby. So great was the freestanding rock that legend attributed its deposition there to the Biblical Flood. The farm was owned by the Wilkinson family, which consisted of mother, father, three brothers and an unknown number of daughters.

We do not know who first saw the Grey Lady, but from the outset her behaviour was remarkably consistent. She would appear after dark on the large rock, which local historians say was situated approximately sixty yards in front of the farmhouse. She would sit there, legs dangling over the edge, wrapped in a grey cloak and sporting a low-browed, black bonnet, the shadow of which eclipsed her eyes.

There is another aspect of the story over which opinions differ. All versions of the tale are unanimous that the presence of the Grey Lady was accompanied by a regular, repetitive knocking noise which sounded as if something was being hammered against the stone upon which the spectre sat. Some versions also declare that the spectre held in her hand a hammer which she constantly raised in the air and brought down upon the rock in between her legs. The latter version sounds more likely to me, as it provides a logical explanation not only for the sound but for its cause.

At first, everyone in the household was terrified when the woman appeared and the ominous-sounding knocking noises began. However, so frequent did her visits become that the family actually became immune to them. Eventually, the servants even plucked up the courage to walk right past the phantom as she banged away on the rock and simply ignored her. Strange though it seems, they became so used to her being there that they scarcely noticed her at all. 'Nellie the Knocker', as they named her, attracted no more attention than a passing swallow or a falling leaf.

Now the two oldest brothers, who were 'approaching manhood' according to some accounts, seem to have taken a special interest in Nellie the Knocker, as indeed did one servant. Moses Aaron Richardson in his 1845 book, *The Local Historian's Table Book, Vol. II* makes the most enigmatic statement imaginable – one which certainly hints at more than we are explicitly told – when he says that Nellie's dress,

> *... varied not with the vicissitudes of seasons'*, and that a certain servant, *'pried sympathetically into the progress of her monotonous occupation; and though her pale, ghastly, contracted features, gave a momentary pang of terror – that unhinged the courage of the boldest – it was rapidly effaced, in the vortex of good fellowship, into which he was speedily drawn. Did the lover venture an appointment with his mistress at the rustic style of the stack-garth? Nelly's unwearied hammer, instead of proving a barrier, only served by imparting a grateful sense of mutual danger, to render more intense the raptures of the hour of meeting.*

The sexual undertones are obvious here, and Richardson is clearly hinting that the servant and Nellie the Knocker embarked upon an intense if bizarre affair, and that the incessant *tap, tap, tap* of her hammer upon the rock only served to heighten the man's physical anticipation.

The brothers, on the other hand, appear to have taken an interest in Nellie the Knocker for less romantic reasons. It seemed to them that her incessant, nocturnal knocking had a purpose to it;

specifically, to draw their attention to something. But what? There had long been rumours that treasure was buried on the farm somewhere; a legacy from ages past, the origins of which were now covered by the sands of time. Was Nellie trying to direct the brothers to its location? The more they thought about it, the more appealing the idea became. They decided to approach their father about the matter. On reflection he agreed that Nellie may indeed be trying to help them find the legendary treasure but where was it buried? How on earth could the spectre's incessant rapping be of any value as a clue?

It was one of the brothers who had a eureka moment and suggested that the treasure may have been buried under the very rock itself. Perhaps Nellie's repeated bringing down of the hammer upon the rock was a visual clue. Perhaps symbolically she was saying, 'Smash this rock!'

What further part the father played in the matter is uncertain, but it was the two older brothers alone who put the plan into action. The maid was given the day off and the rest of the family diverted elsewhere until only the two siblings were left at the farm. Then, with the aid of a considerable amount of explosive material, they blew the rock to smithereens. When the dust settled, the brothers began to dig into the earth and there they found several earthenware vessels filled with gold. How they explained away the disappearance of the rock we do not know, but they managed to keep their find a closely-guarded secret. The fortune was used to expand the farm, and the family lived in comfort for the rest of their days. At some point they must have told of how they came upon their good fortune, of course, for how else would we know of it now?

There is one final mystery that needs our attention, however – how did the jars full of gold find their way beneath a colossal rock which had, according to Biblical chronology, sat there for roughly 4,000 years? Perhaps only Nellie the Knocker could have answered that question, but unfortunately she was never seen again once her throne of stone had been demolished.

The Splitback Demon

The north of England has a long and hallowed tradition when it comes to stories of monsters or, to give the subject its proper title, cryptozoology. Cryptozoology is, for the uninitiated, the study of unknown or mystery animals. Generally, when the topic of mystery animals rears its head, one thinks of the Yeti, Bigfoot or the Loch Ness Monster. In fact, Northumberland plays host to a veritable legion of strange critters which are every bit as exotic – and enigmatic – as their counterparts in far-flung climes. The Beast of Bolam Lake, the Laidley Worm of Spindleston Heugh (see chapter 26) and others have helped to establish Northumberland as the jewel in the cryptozoological crown of the British Isles. Many people have heard these tales and enthusiastically perpetuated them over a pint in their local pub, but few know that Northumberland is also home to a bizarre swamp monster known as the Splitback Demon.

In the summer of 2008, a rambler was out walking at an undisclosed location in Northumberland – I have since established with some certainty that it was not too far from the town of Hexham – when he saw something run across his field of vision and dive into a bog. He described the creature as five feet in height, brown/green in colour and scaled. The beast was essentially anthropomorphic – that is, human-looking – but it also possessed a tail, had no discernible ears and sported a reddish, serrated crest upon its head and spine. Its face was, said the rambler, 'snout-like' and resembled that of a German Shepherd dog in shape.

Now, this rambler didn't mind me telling the world about his encounter with 'the thing', providing that I didn't release his name. He was very reluctant to have this splashed all over the papers as he felt that it wouldn't do his career prospects much good. Trust me, if you knew what he did for a living, you'd understand why. I have given him my solemn word not to divulge his personal details to anyone until he feels it's appropriate to do so.

He struck me as a perfectly reliable witness. What threw me completely, though, was being contacted by a second witness less than two weeks later who claimed to have seen the very same beast – or at least, something very close to it. This time, the witness managed to keep the creature in view for around two minutes.

Normally I'm a trusting soul, but I couldn't help but be suspicious. It wasn't so much that two people claimed to have seen the same creature that bothered me, but the location of the second sighting. It was literally miles away from the first location and, by no stretch of the imagination could I conceive that the same animal could have moved from one to the other place without being spotted many times. Either it had to be a different beast of the same species, or, just possibly, I was being set up to look like an idiot. Another problem was the nature of the second location; it just seemed the most unlikely place for some sort of lizard-like creature to be living. Still, in the weird and wonderful world of cryptozoology, you never can tell. After all, the woods at Bolam Lake aren't much bigger than my front lawn, but there was a hairy hominid dodging about in there for months.

I contacted the first man again and asked him to relate his sighting for a second time in greater detail. Sometimes, investigators can glean important clues on the second recitation that were either not mentioned the first time around or accidentally missed. His account is as follows:

One Sunday in July 2008, Witness A left his home in Northumberland and drove to a remote spot in the north to engage in a spot of rambling. He arrived at his destination and parked his car at approximately 10.40 am, and then walked up a path which took him between two small hillocks. In his backpack were a flask of tea and a packet of biscuits. After walking between the hillocks, the chap came across a large area covered with scrub, and scattered amongst it were a number of 'small, boggy areas filled with peat'. He noticed that as he walked forward the ground was becoming increasingly waterlogged and spongy. Suddenly, to his right, he saw what he at first thought was a man running across the ground 'at high speed'. He estimates that he was approximately twenty yards away from him, and was puzzled as he could not see where he had come from.

'He seemed to come out of nowhere', the witness told me, 'as if he had suddenly popped up out of the ground'. The man also told me that the creature – by that point he'd realised that it certainly wasn't human – had a gait that was perfectly human-like. 'There wasn't anything funny about the way he ran. If it hadn't been for his strange appearance, I would have thought it was just a man.'

Within seconds the creature had crossed the path of Witness A and gave no indication of being aware that he was not alone. It was, said the witness, 'as if I wasn't there'. The chap also recalled seeing occasional splashes of water near the creature's feet as it disturbed the boggy ground beneath it. Then, without warning, he claimed that it, 'just seemed to sink into the ground, as if it had fallen into a hole. There was no noise or anything … it just disappeared.'

Witness A then retraced his steps, found his car and proceeded to drive home. His ramble had been of incredibly short duration, but the incident had removed any desire to prolong it. He said that although the creature had not threatened him or even looked in his direction, he was extremely frightened. He remembers his heart beating incredibly fast and said that his mouth dried up so much that, even if he'd wanted to speak or shout, he would have been unable to.

The creature, which I have been told is known as the Splitback Demon (although up till this juncture I only had the testimony of a singular Northumbrian regarding this) looks pretty much like a cross between a 1950s 'B' movie reject and a diminutive Godzilla. Still, as cryptids go, that'll do for me. To be honest, and to quote Alice, the tale just gets curiouser and curiouser.

The Splitback Demon is (or seems to be) a bizarre cross between human and reptile. According to Witness B, as well as a mane of vivid-red hair, long tail and a rather ostentatious spinal fin, the Splitback Demon also sports two red, glowing eyes, scaly skin, and four-inch long talons.

I rapidly came to the conclusion that there was definitely a degree of credibility to these two eye-witness testimonies. And here's another funny thing, as if lizardy-type personages running around the Northumbrian peat bogs wasn't funny enough, it has recently come to my attention that around the time Witness B, as he prefers to be called, espied his lizard-man, another unconnected witness had an extremely odd UFO encounter at exactly the same location. Later, there would be others. I really didn't want to go down the UFO-reptilian route with my research, as I've hitherto thought it to be a load of old baloney, but I wouldn't be much of an investigator if I deliberately turned down the opportunity to glean insight into the matter simply because it didn't juxtapose well with my philosophical leanings. The truth is that the location where Witness B saw his lizard-man is so obscure and remote that two unconnected Fortean encounters occurring there at the same time is a hard concept for me to swallow.

So, determined to get to the bottom of the enigma, I appealed for other witnesses, if indeed there were any, to come forward. As word started to spread that I was looking for anyone – and indeed anything – connected with the Splitback Demon, a small but steady trickle of leads started to flow in my direction. Some were obviously false, like the one from a 'park ranger' who claimed that an entire family of the creatures was living at Jesmond Dene, and 'working to take over the world'– an outlandish theory, but theoretically not impossible, except for the fact that they were supposedly in league with the Antichrist. That, for me, was a step too far. I'm as broadminded as they come, but even I have my limits.

Astonishingly, another correspondent claimed that the Splitback Demon had impregnated her and, in three months' time, the offspring of their 'close encounter' would be making its entrance into the world. The midwife's face would have been a picture, had she been telling the truth.

For a number of weeks after, the only other contact was from people who claimed to have either seen the Splitback Demon or, alternatively, 'worked out' where the critters were living and wanted me to organise an expedition into darkest Northumberland to track them down. Most of these were members of local 'paranormal research groups' and it was evident that they saw the Splitback Demon as a means of getting their names up in lights. I was not impressed, and politely but firmly declined their offers.

One day, though, I received a letter from a young lady who was living temporarily in Newcastle-upon-Tyne. Refreshingly, she claimed neither to have seen the Splitback Demon or had sex with it. Further, she made no pretensions to knowing where it lived or what its relationship was, if any, to His Satanic Majesty. Still, Victoria Manley had an intriguing tale to tell. My wife and I met up with her in Newcastle city centre. She was charming, completely comfortable sharing her bizarre story with a complete stranger and, to me, seemed wholly truthful.

Victoria came from what she called 'farming stock'. Her great-grandfather had owned a farm in Norfolk, her grandfather had bred cattle in Wales and her own father had spent years growing grapes in South Africa. 'My family loves the land', she had written in her letter, obviously with some pride.

Victoria said that her mother had been born in Weardale and, after marrying Victoria's father, went to South Africa where the couple made a decent living tending the aforementioned vineyards. They were still there, and had no plans to return to the UK. As for Victoria, she had always wanted to visit her parents' birthplace.

During her trip she had taken the opportunity to look up members of her family, most of whom were complete strangers. One relative, an aunt, lived in Hexham and Victoria decided to pay her a visit. Her aunt had been a widow for a number of years and lived in a small terraced house, the interior of which Victoria described as, 'like an old cottage … wonderful'. Although she had never met Victoria, her aunt bade her welcome and spent three hours with her reminiscing over family members both living and dead. At some point, the aunt asked Victoria if she'd ever heard of Lizzie, a sister of her maternal grandfather. She hadn't, but the old woman proceeded to tell her a fascinating tale about something that had happened to Lizzie as a child.

Seemingly, Lizzie had gone to Northumberland to stay in an old farmhouse for a week with friends of the family. These friends had a daughter called Emily, who was slightly older than Lizzie, and from the outset the two girls were firm friends. One afternoon the youngsters went for a walk and came across a small copse of trees. They were about to enter the copse when Lizzie saw something move. At first she thought it was a dog, but then she saw that it was 'a man with green skin' crouching down in the bushes, as if hiding. Lizzie pointed out the 'man' to Emily, who at first couldn't see him. However, as her eyes focused, she was eventually able to make him out and, without further ado, screamed loudly. The two girls ran all the way home as fast as their legs would carry them.

Victoria had probed her aunt for more details, but none were forthcoming. The aunt wasn't being deliberately obstructive; she simply couldn't think of anything else of relevance to tell her. We asked Victoria what her aunt's view was concerning the incident. She paused and then replied, 'Well, I'm not sure she believed it. My aunt just said "She was a funny one, our Lizzie".' Victoria had asked her what she meant by that, and her aunt replied, 'Well, I ask you – seeing green men.'

The intriguing thing about her aunt's reaction was that she seemed to think Lizzie was, 'a funny one' because she'd claimed to have seen a man with green skin, and therefore her word couldn't be trusted because she was obviously eccentric; a perfectly circular argument that gets us nowhere. Had Lizzie carried a history of behaving strangely or seeing weird things, then her aunt's stance might have carried some weight, but she hadn't. She had, by all accounts, been a quite ordinary child who, just one time in her life, had seen something rather extraordinary.

It is unfortunate indeed that we do not know just where the sighting took place. Had it been in the vicinity of the one experienced by Witness A, it would circumstantially add up to something. Northumberland is a big place, however.

Victoria sent me a photograph of herself and said she had no problem with me identifying her. Two weeks later I tried to contact her to see if it might be possible for me to interview her aunt, but her mobile phone number was no longer active. Perhaps she'd returned to South Africa, I don't know.

After meeting with Victoria and reviewing many other cases in my files – cases which touched upon a wide variety of different phenomena – I became convinced of several things. I believe that there truly was a lizard man of some kind in Northumberland, bizarre though the story is, and that there is a subtle but distinct connection between the appearance of the lizard man and other phenomena that had been reported not only in the north-east of England but elsewhere. Questions abound. Who or what was the lizard man, or Splitback Demon? Where did the UFOs that had been seen at the same location come from? And what about the dozens of other strange entities that have also been reported? What explanations could shed light upon them? My questions are still unanswered, but there is no doubt in my mind that near Hexham in Northumberland, a creature called the Splitback Demon lurks …

12

Dreams of a Ghost Ship

The following tale was sent to me by my colleague, Wearside's venerable investigator of all things strange and mysterious, Allan Tedder. The witness in the case wishes to remain anonymous so, for the duration of the story, we'll refer to her simply as Grace.

Grace had a happy childhood. Her father found himself working in several different locations in the north-east, including South Shields, Durham City, Houghton-le-Spring and, briefly at one point, Longframlington. It was here, in this picturesque village, that Grace's grandfather related a strange narrative to her back in the 1940s. It is intriguing to say the least.

Grace's maternal grandfather, Bill, had spent all his years in the Merchant Navy. A lifelong sailor, the sea was in his blood. The concept of being a landlubber was something that sent shivers down his spine. 'He never did anything else, never *wanted* to do anything else', said Grace.

'Sometime during 1923, my grandfather was sailing through the Tasman Sea near Australia. The cargo ship he was on was called *The Trinidad*, if I remember rightly, although I don't recall what he said they were transporting. On one occasion there was a terrible storm, and Grandfather told me that for a while he thought they might even sink. They didn't, but it was a close thing.

'Eventually the storm died down, but it was still quite windy and the sea was very choppy. At some point Grandfather looked out and saw what he described as a sailing ship bearing down towards them. He panicked and alerted the captain. According to Grandfather, the sailing ship got ever closer, but didn't crash into *The Trinidad*. It just sailed past.'

The intriguing thing was that, according to old Bill, the sails were ragged and the creaking, moulding vessel appeared as if it had been floating around the ocean for decades. At no time did Bill or any of his colleagues see any sailors aboard the ship. Grace also recalled her grandfather telling her that the ship's captain had made no attempt to contact the ghostly vessel, the name of which she thought may have been the *Breda*, although she couldn't be sure. I wondered if this might have been due to the superstitious nature of sailors but later, on reflection, I concluded that what probably made the captain most suspicious was the fact that the vessel was an old-fashioned sailing ship.

But this wasn't quite the end of the tale. The eerie ship sailed off into the night and Bill, along with his shipmates, retired to his bunk to rest his weary frame. As the grizzled mariner waited for sleep to overtake him, he suddenly became aware that someone – or to be more specific, something – was in the cabin beside him. 'It was a presence', he told his granddaughter, 'that's the only way I can describe it'. According to Bill, he immediately opened his eyes and saw what he described as 'the ghostly form of an old sailor' standing in the corner by a locker.

'Grandfather said he was a captain' claimed Grace, 'because of his brass-buttoned jacket and cap. He didn't say anything. He just stood staring for a while and then faded away.'

The obvious question, of course, was whether the ghost that appeared to Bill was in some way connected to the spectral sailing vessel that had passed them earlier that evening. 'Grandfather never found out', Grace told me, 'but he said the ghost didn't frighten him in any way. He never forgot the incident and recited it to me frequently as a child.'

Eventually, the entire family relocated to Blyth – Bill's home town. Bill had moved in permanently with his daughter, son-in-law and Grace by this time, but, Grace believed, the ghostly sailor had joined them. 'My grandfather often felt the presence of the sailor ghost, particularly in the last years of his life. He never admitted to seeing him, but my mother and I were convinced that he had. We could be walking down the High Street, and he'd suddenly stop and stare across the road, as if he was looking at someone. He'd smile, and then walk on …'

13

The Legend of Cutty Soames

Before delving into the legend of Cutty Soames – and there is indeed a fascinating legend to delve into, I promise you – we first need to look at the context in which the tale is set, for it has been subjected to many misunderstandings and misapprehensions over the centuries.

Until the 18th century, coal mines or 'pits' were just that, holes or pits in the ground, sometimes open-cast, at which even monks and millers would take their turn hewing the 'black gold' for fuel. By the time of the Industrial Revolution, however, the need for coal had rocketed and mining was becoming big business. It was also a dangerous business. The build-up of flammable gases would cause explosions, roof collapses would bury many alive, and flooding took the lives of more than a few. Incredibly, women – even pregnant women – and small children were expected to work in such vile conditions.

From time-to-time, efforts were made to improve things. Primitive ventilation techniques were attempted – with varying degrees of success. Regulations were introduced to make support props a minimum thickness and maximum shift lengths were applied to pregnant women and very young children.

Children were not, of course, expected to do the work of a fully-grown adult. Some, known as trappers, would be ensconced in small recesses, their role being to open and shut doors so that the coal tubs could move unhindered. They were also trained how to regulate the flow of air through the mines by the same method – an incredible responsibility for a young child.

As the children matured, their work down the pit changed. They would eventually become hurriers or thrusters; that is, responsible for pulling and pushing the incredibly heavy coal tubs through the mine. Pushing the tubs – the job of the thrusters – was a gruelling but relatively simple task. Pulling them – the role of the hurrier – was another matter. Hurriers whose job it was to pull the tubs were fitted with a Soames harness; a robust jacket attached to the tub by a rope. As the thruster pushed and the hurrier pulled, momentum would be gained and the tub would begin its journey. Sometimes, up to a fifth of youngsters under the age of twelve employed in a mine could die of injuries incurred during their arduous work.

The dark, dank conditions down the mine, coupled with the poor lighting conditions, naturally lent themselves to ghost stories, and almost every coal pit was believed to be haunted. Small, blue flames would often be seen darting hither and thither; these were believed to be the legendary Blue Caps, sprites which lived underground. Also said to be present in some mines were the Kobolds (from the word 'cobalt') who would manipulate the potentially dangerous mineral they were named after and put miners at risk.

And then there were the elves, the most feared of which was the legendary Cutty Soames. Readers will have already noticed the similarity between the moniker of this elemental creature and the harness that young hurriers were required to wear. This is not coincidental. This venomous elf was more accurately known as the Soames Cutter, but over time this was bastardised to 'Cutty Soames'.

So, just what sort of tricks did Cutty Soames get up to? He was, if you'll excuse the pun, something of a one-trick pony down the mine. His modus operandi was to cut the rope attaching the Soames harness worn by the hurrier to the coal tub. Sometimes he would do this when the harness was empty; that is, not being worn by a hurrier. The mineworkers would suddenly find the rope or *soam* severed, fine strands of it scattered around the earth like confetti. Their work would be delayed. On some occasions, however, he was said to have cut the soams of hurriers whilst they were actively pulling tubs. This had little effect on the hurrier, who would merely stumble forward, but the consequences for the thruster at the rear could be disastrous if the tub suddenly careered backwards.

Goblins also inhabited the pits, by tradition in packs of seven, and would often take pity on the miners and attempt to warn them of the presence of Cutty Soames or other malign entities. They would make piercing whistling sounds as an alarm, hence they were often referred to as the Seven Whistlers.

Cutty Soames was said to visit a number of pits, but his true home was the mine at Shilbottle. Here, it seems, his demeanour was more mercurial. He went about his usual business, but sometimes he seemed to take pity on the miners, particularly if they were feeling the brunt of the callousness of the mine owners. He would hide valuable pieces of machinery, smear excrement on their clothing and engage in other kinds of naughtiness, which the miners infinitely preferred to his normal habit of soam-cutting.

There were times when doubt was cast upon the existence of Cutty Soames. Some suggested that the soam-cutting was the work of a deranged miner, and there were several instances when the circumstantial evidence did seem to point in that direction. One tale in currency concerns a pit deputy from Cramlington. His colleagues noticed that Cutty Soames never seemed to go about his business when the deputy was off-shift, and they suspected that it was he, and not Cutty who was doing the cutting. The deputy, by tradition called Nelsham (or, as in one version I have seen, Nelson), grew tired of the allegations, which he claimed were false, and decided to seek revenge on his accusers. He plotted to do this in the most chilling way imaginable. Before going off-shift, he cut the soam on one of the tubs used to take the miners down to the coal face, leaving it intact by only one thread. His plan was that the following morning his two main accusers would climb into the tub – the one they normally used. The extra weight would then cause the last strand of the soam to snap, allowing the tub to hurtle downwards at breakneck speed, carrying the men to their deaths.

The plan worked – in a fashion. The only problem was that the man's main accusers were delayed, thus causing two other miners to use the sabotaged tub. They died horribly, whilst the intended targets escaped. According to legend, virtually everyone believed that the deputy had knobbled the tub that carried the men to their deaths. Outraged, they decided to avenge them. Several days passed, and then a mysterious fire broke out. Nelsham (or, if you like, Nelson) was burnt to death.

I've tried to find reference to these incidents, but have failed. As one of the nearby pits at Cramlington was actually named Nelson Colliery, I suspect that the name of the alleged deputy may have arisen out of some confusion between the two. Still, questions remain. Did Cutty Soames slice the ropes for which the deputy was unfairly blamed? Or was it the deputy all along? Did the deputy subsequently cut the soam on the tub which resulted in the death of two innocent miners? And why did the two main accusers of the deputy not take their usual place in the first tub that morning?

We may never know, but Cutty Soames might …

14

The Scent of Blood

Some years ago I held a competition for readers of my *WraithScape* column in *The Shields Gazette.* Quite simply, the best supernatural story submitted, as judged by myself and a journalist from the newspaper, would receive a free bottle of wine and an attractive calendar produced by a well-known local paranormal research group, Avalon Skies. The prizes were modest, the stories submitted superb.

Making the decision as to which story deserved to be on top of the pile wasn't easy, but eventually we settled upon the following one submitted by a reader who wished only to be known as Roz. It was duly published, although not with as much detail as the version below, and elicited quite a reaction from readers, one or two of whom said they'd had similar experiences themselves.

Roz's account wasn't the most dramatic I'd ever heard, and nor was it the goriest. Ostensibly, in fact, there was nothing about it at all which would chill the blood and it definitely wasn't a prime candidate to be made into a horror movie. However, as the journalist and I agreed, there was something subtly eerie about it and it was – this time not so subtly – very macabre indeed.

'One sunny July morning in the summer of 1998', Roz related, 'my husband, son and I decided to go out for the day. We didn't know exactly where we were going to; we just liked driving around. We used to do that a lot … drive up to the A1 and then decide whether to head north or south.'

Roz said that although she wouldn't describe herself as psychic, there had been odd moments in her life when she'd had premonitions, presentiments regarding the future. They'd never concerned things of great import, but nevertheless Roz hadn't been in any doubt about their veracity. She'd get a feeling that something was about to happen and, inevitably, it would. I asked Roz if she'd had any premonition that the day in question would turn out to be so absolutely wretched, but she said no. She had had no idea what was in store. Here is her account:

'The day started out fine and everyone was happy. We were just so enjoying driving around. We headed south and ended up in Weardale. As far as I can recall, we stopped for a pub lunch somewhere, and we enjoyed that too.'

So far so good, then. Whilst Roz and her family were touring Weardale, another family member was also setting off on a road journey. This one was not to have such a happy ending, as we shall see.

Roz takes up the story again:

'After lunch we were driving along quite happily, when suddenly the interior of the car was filled with the awful smell of blood. The weird thing was that I could smell it but nobody else could.'

When the story was subsequently published in my column, I commented that, with hindsight, the fact that the smell was so strong and yet no one else could detect it was probably a sign that something beyond the rational was occurring. Now, however, I'm a bit older and wiser, and I'm not so sure I was right. Sometimes people have subjective experiences – experiences that no one else seems to be sharing at the time – for a number of reasons. In this case, it could have simply been that Roz's husband didn't have as acute a sense of smell as his spouse. Then again, certain illnesses such as the common cold can cause people to 'smell' and 'taste' things subjectively; that is, the sensations have no objective reality, and are purely the result of physiological processes going on within the body.

'This went on all afternoon', says Roz, 'but no matter what I did, I couldn't get rid of that smell. It was just so strong'.

The hours passed. Apart from the persistent smell of blood, Roz says, the day went really well. The odour disturbed her, though. 'I think what bothered me is that blood has a smell like nothing else. When you smell blood, you know it's blood and not something else … it has that bitter, copper-like smell that you only get with blood.'

Disturbing though the odour was, Roz told herself that there must have been a rational explanation for it. However, any thoughts she may have had along this line well and truly evaporated after the family arrived back home.

'After we got home I made the tea, but even then I could still smell the blood. I just couldn't understand it.'

And then the telephone rang – a call which Roz now wishes she'd never had had to answer.

'It was my mother. She'd called to say that my cousin had been killed in a motorbike accident that very afternoon. As soon as I put the telephone down I noticed that the strong smell of blood had gone away completely.'

After Roz contacted the *Gazette* with her story I decided that I should interview her personally. I met with both her and her husband one Wednesday evening in the basement bar of a local pub, and over a beer listened intently as she related her feelings about that fateful day. She recalled something odd in addition to the strange odour of blood that had followed her around for hours.

'That morning', Roz recalled, 'when we went for our drive, we decided to head south on a whim. We could just as easily have headed north. In fact, we toyed with the idea. Had we, I think we'd have probably ended up in Rothbury as we'd actually discussed the possibility of going there. The terrible thing is that it was just outside of Rothbury where my cousin died.'

Had they decided to visit Rothbury instead of Weardale, Roz and her husband worked out, they would have almost certainly been travelling along the same road where her cousin died at approximately the same time. In fact, it's entirely possible that they could have witnessed the accident or its aftermath. Roz wondered whether something had taken a hand in making sure that didn't happen by subconsciously prompting them to travel in the other direction. True or not, one can certainly sympathise with her for thinking along those lines.

But what of that awful, clinging odour of blood that affected Roz so much? A sign, perhaps, that, on another road in another county, a loved family member was tragically ending their earthly sojourn?

'It was the worst smell I have ever smelt in my life', she said, 'and I hope I don't ever get it again.'

15

The Blacksmith Healer

Over the years I've investigated many stories involving healers who use unconventional methods of relieving the sick of their ailments. Some of them have been truly bizarre, such as the travelling 'dentist' in the Philippines who removed rotten teeth by slapping his patients, and the Scots 'physic' who cured stomach ailments by blowing pepper into the faces of his patients – one hopes with their eyes firmly shut. Not all of these folk-cures work, of course, but, considering their often strange nature, a surprising number of them do.

There have been folk-cures in the past that didn't seem to make scientific sense at the time, but which were later found to have a degree of validity. But what about treatments that seem so bizarre that they simply cannot be justified by any rational means whatsoever? Well, you may be surprised to learn that, quite often, they work, too.

In the 18th and 19th centuries, there used to be a belief – widespread in Northumberland – that infected wounds caused by rusty metal could be treated not by visiting the local doctor, but by employing the services of a blacksmith. Intrigued? Then read on.

In the 1880s, so the story goes, a young farm-hand from Stamfordham was asked to cut back some briar bushes at the side of the road. As he sliced back and forth with the scythe, he misjudged his swing and his hand glanced over the top of a fencepost. From the top of the post protuded a rusty nail, and the nail ripped through the flesh of the lad's little finger and the lower fleshy part of his hand. Blood instantly ran from the wound. Of course, infection from tetanus – often referred to as lockjaw back then, due to its symptoms – was a big conern. Hence, when the farm-hand went home and mentioned the wound to his father, his father demanded to take a closer look. He was disturbed to see that a part of the rusty nail had actually broken off and was protruding from the wound. Knowing the potentially fatal consequences of leaving such a gash untreated – in fact, it may already have been too late – he immediately removed the nail and then went to the place where the accident had occurred. There, he removed the remainder of the nail from the fencepost and took both pieces to the local blacksmith who happened to be working at the local jail. Some might wonder why he didn't take his son to the doctor instead, as that would have seemed to be the more logical course of action, but the father knew exactly what he was doing.

The blacksmith, on being presented with the parts of the nail, examined them and then promptly set to work. He carefully removed every trace of rust and polished them until they were gleaming like … well, like a new nail, I suppose. The young lad's wound promptly healed and never bothered him again.

Reapers near the Scottish Borders would, if they accidentally cut themselves with their sickle, immediately polish it in the belief that to clean the sickle would also clean the wound. Surely there could be no justification for this belief, could there? How on earth could anyone imagine that cleaning a piece of metal could affect the sanitisation of an infected wound? Nonsense!

Well, I'm not so sure. I'd agree that anyone who cuts themselves on rusty metal needs to seek medical advice, particularly if they aren't up to date with their tetanus jabs. Not for one moment am I suggesting that anyone who could be infected with tetanus should refrain from promptly seeking medical help or refuse treatment. But, of course, there *were* no such treatments back then, so what made people think that cleaning and polishing the rusty artefact that cut you would help?

My guess, and that's all it is, is that the power of the mind can affect the body in ways that we haven't even discovered yet, and that a consuming belief that something will work may actually cause it to. If people back then – people like the farm-hand and his father – had absolute faith in some of these folk-cures, perhaps the strength of their belief was enough to make the body heal itself.

One of the signs that an old folk-cure may have been effective in days of yore was its prevalence. In fact, a similar belief existed in the southern counties of England. In Cornwall, a farmer once found a rusty nail embedded in the ankle of his pony. He carefully pulled the nail out, discarded it and only then went to consult the blacksmith. When the blacksmith was told that the man had thrown the nail away, he berated him. How on earth could he effect a cure by polishing the nail if he didn't have it to work on? The pony later succumbed to infection and died.

There are many other old Northumbrian folk-remedies which work on the same principle. For instance, there is a common belief that burying a piece of meat in the ground can cure warts. As the meat rots away, so the idea goes, the wart rots too and eventually drops off. My maternal grandmother tried it several times in her younger days, and swore that it worked every time. Why? Because she truly believed it would.

16

The Singing Ghost of Thirlwall Castle

Thirlwall Castle is a somewhat dilapidated but nevertheless picturesque 12th-century edifice which stands on a bank of the River Tipalt, near the village of Greenhead. Like most castles of its kind, it has undergone significant changes over the centuries. The castle was fortified in 1828 by John Thirlwall and, as with St Paul's church at Jarrow and other buildings of historical significance, local masons made good use of stones already cut and shaped by Roman builders of a previous era. These were transported from the Roman Wall and incorporated into Thirlwall Castle with great skill.

For centuries, Thirlwall Castle was a local jewel in the crown of Northumberland. However, by the mid 15th century, things had begun to change. John Thirlwall, the then owner, had maintained the castle, but that was about the most charitable thing that could be said about its condition. Not long after, the luck of the Thirlwall family was blighted by the death of Sir Percival Thirlwall. Percival was killed at the Battle of Bosworth Field on 22nd August, 1485. He was King Richard's standard-bearer there and legend has it that, bravely, he held the Yorkist standard high, even after having his legs cut away by a Tudor broadsword.

By the mid 17th century, the roofs had started to sag, the gates had begun to fall away from their brackets and rust was slowly eating away at what had once been polished iron and steel.

The last of the Thirlwall line was Eleanor, who in 1738 married one Matthew Swinburne of Capheaton Hall. The castle remained in the hands of the Swinburnes for merely a decade before it was sold to the Earl of Carlisle for £4,000.

By 1832 much of the castle was a shambles and part of it actually collapsed. Further collapses occurred, eventually resulting in the Northumberland National Park Authority taking over the management of the building to protect it from further decay. Happily, Thirlwall Castle was granted Grade I Listed Building status and Scheduled Ancient Monument status.

That such an edifice would be devoid of ghosts, or at least ghost stories, is unthinkable. Hence I was delighted when my good friend and colleague John Triplow told me of his own experience there.

In late 2008, John was contacted by photographer and researcher Gail Ward, a mutual friend of both John and myself. In fact, it was Gail who first brought the Thirlwall ruin to John's attention. Gail told John some of the tales attached to Thirlwall – tales of spectres and shadowy phantoms. Intrigued, John decided to contact the owners of the property in the hope that they would grant both he and Gail access to the site so that they could conduct an investigation there. Magnanimously, they assented.

In February 2009, John and his partner, Kelly Williams, arranged to meet with Gail before heading over to Thirlwall Castle. John recalls that the weather conditions were less than optimum, to put it mildly. In fact, during the previous week, much of mainland U.K. had been hit by snowstorms and blizzards. Regardless, they soldiered on. Shortly after their arrival, darkness began to set in.

As the night wore on, Gail reported that she was being repeatedly distracted by what sounded like a female singing. Now John is a balanced and objective researcher. He strained to hear the ghostly voice that had riveted Gail's attention, but he could not. In fact, John told me that, '… what Gail had described was fascinating, but my gut instinct was that she was hearing a combination of the nearby Tipalt Burn that runs rapidly by one side of the castle and other background sounds. Together, I believed, they could well be causing an illusion that almost sounded like the faint echoing of a female voice.'

By 3 am the cold had become unbearable and the investigators decided to call an end to their vigil. Kelly, Gail and John rambled down the side of the hill towards a narrow gravel path which would take them to where they'd parked their car. John takes up the story:

'We had only walked about twenty metres or so along the path before the three of us stopped dead in our tracks. Open-mouthed, we stared at each other and simultaneously blurted out, "What the hell was that?". The reason was that we had all heard a loud, distinctly female voice boom from within the castle, and she was singing! Thankfully, I had left my recorder running during that time and successfully managed to capture the strange, ethereal voice.'

There is an intriguing postscript to this tale. When John analysed his recording, he discovered that he had recorded the mystery voice not once, but *twice*.

'In retrospect', he told me, 'I think I was honoured to have experienced what I did. I only hope that one day – or night – I will encounter something of a similar nature again. To be honest, I found the whole experience very touching.'

17

The Grey Ghost of Cresswell

Another tale I have to thank my colleague John Triplow for is that of the Grey Ghost of Cresswell. It's one of those fascinating stories which, for reasons we can only guess at, never seems to gain currency far from its setting. That truly is a shame, I think, for like John, I find it captivating.

Cresswell is a small village in Northumberland which lies not too far to the north of Ashington. It sits upon the coast, looking out over the tempestuous North Sea. The contrast between the roar of the sea and the silence of Cresswell at dawn couldn't be more striking. The village draws tourists like a magnet, despite its diminutive size, as is amply proven by the fact that it plays host to no less than two caravan parks. Nearby is the cosy bay of Snab Point which – some would say unfortunately – is overshadowed by a large aluminium smelting plant just to the south. It also draws geologists both amateur and professional, for the adjacent beach is littered with pieces of fossilised wood, much of it having detached itself from the cliffs nearby. The cliffs themselves date back to the Carboniferous period, some 350 million years ago. In every respect, then, Cresswell and its surroundings are truly of ancient provenance.

Several years ago, John found himself becoming increasingly intrigued by the folklore surrounding Cresswell. He started to collect eyewitness testimonies of people who had seen bizarre animals, ghosts, UFOs and other paranormal phenomena in the area. 'There was even an alleged alien abduction there, once', he told me.

One tale seemed to catch John's attention more than the others, though, and he put out an appeal in a local magazine, *A Creeful of Coals*, asking readers if they had any personal recollections of it. His goal? To find out the truth about the Grey Ghost (or Grey Lady) of Cresswell.

It seems that during the early 1940s there was a young girl in Ashington by the name of Margaret Moffett. Margaret was employed by a local lad called Jimmy Padredi, who ran a small family bakery in Cresswell. Now Margaret's normal routine was to get up very early each morning and make her way from Ashington to Cresswell on foot. Sometimes, though, if she managed to get to the village of Ellington in time, she'd hitch a lift with the pit men heading back to Cresswell after finishing their shift at Ellington Colliery.

On one particularly inclement morning – a thick fog had settled – Margaret boarded the 'tanky', as the pit men called their carriage. As the vehicle headed along Cresswell Road towards St Bartholomew's church, something astonishing happened. Margaret, along with several of the miners, suddenly saw the ghostly form of a woman as it walked across the road. The spectre then simply faded away.

What struck Margaret as distinctly odd was the fact that the pit men seemed completely unfazed by the incident and, after a momentary pause, simply carried on talking. There was a very good reason for this. It wasn't the first time they had seen her. The Grey Ghost of Cresswell, sometimes described as wearing a flowing, grey dress, had in fact been espied many times before. It wouldn't be the last time that Margaret Moffett would see the Grey Ghost of Cresswell either.

Not that many days after her first glimpse of the Grey Ghost, Margaret turned up for work as normal. Jimmy Padredi was loading up his cart with freshly-baked goods in preparation for making the morning deliveries. Margaret, as usual, planned to accompany him. The employer and his employee were just about to set off when, without warning, the horse whinnied alarmingly, reared up and then galloped off in the opposite direction to the one they normally took.

Naturally, Jimmy Padredi wanted to know what had spooked his horse so badly. So did Margaret. As they both turned to peer down the road, they were flabbergasted to see none other than the grey-gowned Ghost of Cresswell, hovering there gracefully, just before she faded into the mist.

Years later, after Margaret had married and had children, she would often reminisce about her two encounters with the ghost. Unfortunately, she passed out of this life in 1999, and so can no longer regale friends and family alike with her memories. Till the day she died, however, she was resolute in her claim that what she had seen was nothing more and nothing less than the Grey Lady of Cresswell.

18

The Standing Deer

Back in 1808, an extremely strange thing happened, and it happened at Bamburgh,

There were two men, quarrymen to be exact, and their role was to take large stones and pound them into smaller ones. This probably wasn't the most exciting of pursuits, I'll grant you, but in 1808 one's main concern was having a job, not being picky and choosy over exactly what that employment entailed. Times were different then.

Now at some point the quarrymen were faced with the task of destroying an unusually large boulder, and this necessitated them digging underneath it to a considerable depth. As they did so, one of them uncovered a set of deer antlers. Further digging uncovered the skull, which was still attached to the rest of the skeleton. The two men were joined by several colleagues who, curious, joined them in the dig. They too started to unearth deer antlers, all attached to complete skeletons beneath them. At some point the incredible truth dawned upon them: the deer had all been buried in a standing position, almost as if they had been alive when the earth had covered them.

Eventually, word reached the foreman of the quarry, who attended the scene. He instructed all digging to stop and an expert was called in. Just what sort of expert, contemporary records do not say, but his expertise was enough at least for him to determine that the remains were those of red deer.

Unfortunately, almost as soon as the bones were exposed to the air, they started to crumble. There is a chemical process involved in this which is well understood now, but was little understood in the year 1808. As one local historian observed, 'They mouldered and fell in pieces'. However, for whatever reason, two horns – both about three feet in length – stubbornly refused to succumb to such elemental exposure and remained in good condition. The quarrymen carted them off to Bamburgh Castle where they were hung upon a wall. For all I know, they may still be there to this day.

Now the presence of several deer skeletons (accounts vary, but place the figure between five and nine) buried in such a strange manner is odd enough, but there's more. The quarry workers all stated that the ground in which the deer were found emitted a foul odour of decayed flesh. Now I don't know for how long carcasses buried in the ground smell, but my guess is not for too long, certainly not after several decades or centuries. That seems to indicate that the animals hadn't been there that long, although the rapid decay of the bones after exposure would seem to indicate just the opposite. It really is a mystery.

Putting aside the enigma of why the deer had been buried in that particular location, and for how long they'd been there, the main question is why they had been buried at all. It was suggested at the time that the burial may have been part of some satanic ritual, but personally I think it unlikely. More likely, I think, is that it was connected with paganism and that although the ritual is to our modern eyes repugnant, back then its intentions may well have been honourable. Perceptions have a way of altering radically with the passage of time.

19

The Witch Hare

The parish of Whittingham lies in the heart of rural Northumberland, just to the south-west of Alnwick. It mirrors the very essence of peace and tranquillity, and has a wonderful historical heritage. Religiously speaking, the Christian faith has long been the predominant influence in the village. Testimony to this is the architecturally simple but, nonetheless, impressive church of St Bartholomew, which sits opposite an equally picturesque schoolhouse. The history of the church can be traced back to the mid 7th century.

In ancient times, Northumbrian society still played host to various forms of non-Christian spirituality. However, with the slow but steady growth of Christianity, such alternative forms of worship were either driven underground or simply faded away due to unpopularity. Along with them withered some very strange (but not necessarily false) notions, such as the existence of the Witch Hare.

Within the confines of orthodox Christian theology, animals are seen as 'sentient' in a very limited sense. They are aware of things, but do not dream dreams, aspire to greater goals or meditate on philosophical conundrums such as life after death. That's according to Christian theology, of course, but pre-Christian pagans saw things differently. In fact, Druids and other pagans believed that humans could interact with animals in very meaningful ways.

Around Whittingham in the 18th century there was a belief, as in other parts of Northumberland, that if a man met an elderly woman on his way to work, something terrible would happen to him before darkness fell unless he immediately returned home. It beggars belief that such an idea could have been adhered to rigorously, otherwise half the working population would have been constantly walking back and forth and never actually reaching their place of employment. Still, many people did take it seriously, especially, it is said, pit men.

At some point in the historical timeline – we don't know when exactly – the aversion to seeing old women early in the morning was expanded to include hares. No, I haven't a clue why either, but it did. Humorous though it seems, when one imagines how it must have worked in practice, such an idea actually took root. But why?

It was believed that witches had 'familiars'. Familiars were animals (Christians believed them to be demon-possessed) which did the bidding of witches. If a familiar crossed your path, you could be in big trouble. As hares were supposed to be particularly favoured by witches, then they were one animal that you had to pay particular care to stay away from. Some people believed that if you were savvy enough, you could actually tell the difference between ordinary, harmless hares and those in the employ of witches. Familiars were sometimes said to have red eyes/large eyes, unusually long teeth or protruding snouts. In recent years there have been reports of rabbits or hares, some said to be literally the size of cows, which have caused damage to rural communities in Northumberland.

In 2008, I was contacted by store manager Michael Ingham. He told me that in February 2005, he was driving between Glanton and Whittingham when he saw a rabbit or a hare (he wasn't sure which) in the centre of the road. He slowed down to avoid hitting it, but became irritated when the creature stood its ground and simply stared at the vehicle. Michael figured that if he got out of the car the creature might take flight, but he was wrong. It just stared at him. Then, to his astonishment, it started to hop towards him.

'There was something about that thing that bugged me, to be honest. I thought rabbits and hares were supposed to be timid creatures, but this one wasn't. It's embarrassing to admit, but it got me frightened. I just got back in the car as quickly as I could and drove around it. I don't know what it did next, and I didn't hang around to find out.'

It sounds strange to imagine a fully-grown man becoming agitated at the presence of something as small as a hare or a rabbit, but we must remember that this sense of uneasiness has a long historical provenance. Maybe there's something about hares and rabbits – goodness knows what – that just spooks us psychologically under certain circumstances. Did he see Whittingham's very own Witch Hare? We may never know.

20

Fairy Rings

When I was a child, I was told that there were certain ways you could tell whether the fairies had paid you a visit. If you left your tooth under your pillow at night and in the morning it had been replaced by a silver sixpence, then the Tooth Fairy had obviously paid you a visit. The icing sugar on top of your currant bun wasn't really icing sugar at all – it was fairy dust! Most signs that the fairies had paid you a visit were really nothing of the sort; they were simply quaint tales invented by parents to enchant their children – and to explain the presence of that shiny sixpence under the pillow.

But there are other alleged tell-tale signs that the fairies may have been to see you, and some of them were in common currency long before the story about the Tooth Fairy had even been invented. Some, in fact, go back to ancient times. One of them is a very strange phenomenon indeed, commonly known as the 'Fairy Ring'.

Fairies are said to like dancing. As anyone who has ever read a book of children's fairy tales will know, they are believed to dance in circles. Few people claim to have seen fairies dancing, of course, but many claim to have seen the tell-tale signs they've left behind. Fairy rings are, allegedly, the dark circles left on the grass after the fairies have danced there. In some parts of Scandinavia, for example, a belief in fairy rings is taken very seriously and they are viewed with great reverence. Damaging them is thought to bring terrible misfortune to those responsible. Construction firms regularly change their plans to avoid damaging fairy rings, particularly when building highways, as it is believed that to plough a new road through a fairy ring will automatically turn the area into an accident black-spot.

Momentarily making allowances for those who find the concept of circles left by dancing fairies hard to swallow, is there a scientifically acceptable explanation that would make sense to the rationalist? Indeed there is. Whatever the cause, 'such areas should be protected', says lecturer and folklore expert Stephen Swales, 'as Faerie Rings are not common. I would hope that local environmentalists would investigate such sightings and find out exactly what type of natural phenomenon this is'.

Actually, we already have a good idea. Fairy rings are, at least in many cases, caused by a fungus which feeds on nutrients in the grass and in the top centimetre of soil. When the nutrients are exhausted, the small hoop of fungi reaches outwards for a fresh supply. The grass it leaves behind inside the circle then returns to its normal hue. When the new source of nutrients is itself exhausted, the circle of fungi will spread outwards once again in search of sustenance, and so on. This creates an ever-expanding hoop of darker-coloured grass – or, for those who prefer the more exotic explanation – the mysterious Fairy Ring.

Some years ago, north-eastern author Dot Golightly told me she'd found some fairy rings near her home and photographed them. 'I was amazed to see them on the grass next to my house … I didn't know whether to think "alien spaceships" or what?' she quipped.

So, as far as the rationalists are concerned, the whole mystery of fairy rings should be wrapped up, then. In fact, there really seems to be no mystery at all.

But all is not quite what it seems to be in the world of fairy rings, as the following tale relates:

Northumbrian joiner Billy Malone was called to repair a barn near Cragside in the early 1950s. As he walked across a field towards the building he saw an unusual, 'dark, wheel-shaped stain' on the ground – it was none other than a fairy ring.

Now Billy had never seen a fairy ring before. Curious, he veered off course slightly to examine the enigma more closely. 'I didn't think there was anything odd about it really, other than the fact that it was a circle about six feet in width. That seemed rather strange. I thought that something must have been laid on the ground, a wheel of some kind, and made a mark of sorts. The thing is, normally when something is laid on the ground it makes the grass underneath die and it goes paler, not darker.'

Of course, Billy didn't know anything about the fungi that we now accept can cause fairy rings. Had he, he may have simply raised an eyebrow ever so slightly, smiled and moved on. However, as he studied the circle he inadvertently stepped inside it. It was then that something truly extraordinary happened.

'The first thing I felt was dizziness. I was really light-headed. But I could also hear voices singing. They were female voices. I got a bit panicky then, and I just stepped back out the circle and then everything was alright again. I fixed up the side (of the barn) and then left. I just made sure I didn't walk through the ring on the grass again.'

Billy Malone isn't the only person to have had such an experience in a fairy circle. Many people have reported similar sensations of light-headedness, some feeling as if they were even about to faint. Others have reported seeing their skin change colour slightly (normally to a bluish tinge) or seeing small, sparkling lights darting through the air. It is interesting that some people who have strayed into crop circles have reported almost identical phenomena. This opens up some intriguing questions. Is it the peculiar nature of the circles that produces the strange physiological effects, or is it psychosomatic? Are there people who are able to convince themselves that they are undergoing something extremely odd and subsequently imagine the weird symptoms?

Who knows? The majority of fairy circles may indeed have a natural explanation, but not all, as Billy Malone and others will testify.

21

Coming Back for a Memento

When I first wrote up the story you are about to read in one of my newspaper columns many years ago, I began by saying, 'Few people manage to go right throughout their lives without having some sort of paranormal experience, although many people attempt to rationalise strange things that happen to them in an effort to make sense of things which just can't be explained'.

This tale falls right into this category. It begins with a lady called Mary Brown who, during her later years, had lived in Whitburn, South Tyneside. Mary's mother, a resident of Blyth, had died many years previously. She had been held in high regard by everyone who knew her and had been viewed as 'the perfect neighbour'. She had also been a model citizen, serving in the Women's Land Army during the Second World War and was awarded a medal for her service. Mary wasn't been able to recall exactly what her mother's medal had been awarded for, but she did remember that she had treasured it. 'It was something she took great pride in', she said.

When Mary was younger, she and her husband, along with their young son, actually lived in Blyth with her mother. 'The house was small, but there was enough room for everyone and we all got on really well', said Mary. Mary's son was only a toddler when his grandmother died, but he did have fleeting happy memories of her. That, in fact, was why Mary decided it was appropriate to give her son the medal that her mother had been awarded, as a keepsake.

From time to time, the young lad would sit on the sofa with the medal clutched tightly in his hand, staring at it intently. This puzzled me. Was this just a young person's fascination with something old and shiny, or something more? Did looking at the medal help the young lad recall his grandmother? Perhaps, perhaps not. But Mary was adamant that it had held a real fascination for him, whatever the reason.

Mary was concerned that before too long her son's memories would fade, so she often took the time to tell him things about his grandmother in an effort to keep her fresh in his mind. Nevertheless, 'Boys will be boys', as Mary remarked. She used to worry that her son might lose the medal, so she decided to keep it in a cupboard where he couldn't reach it. If he wanted to see the medal, all he had to do was ask Mary and she'd get it for him.

One day, Mary got into conversation with June Kershaw, an elderly neighbour. Mary mentioned to her that her mother had served in the Women's Land Army and was quite surprised to hear that June had also served her country in that way. A thought crossed Mary's mind. She asked June if she would take a look at her mother's medal and, just possibly, be able to tell her under what circumstances it may have been awarded. June said she'd be happy to oblige. Mary went into the house to retrieve the medal from the cupboard but, to her consternation, found it wasn't there. Was it possible that she'd simply forgotten to put it away? No; she clearly recalled replacing it in the cupboard the last time her son had finished looking at it. Frustrated, Mary went outside and told June that she would have to show it to her later.

Mary lost no time in resuming her search. She turned her house upside down, but there was simply no sign of the medal. Finally, Mary decided to go through her son's room; something she should perhaps have done at the beginning. Desperate to find the medal, she began to rummage through cupboards, drawers and boxes. Her son entered the room right in the middle of her efforts.

'Mam, are you looking for Nan's medal?'

'Yes', his mother replied. 'Have you seen it?'

'Yes. Nan came and took it last night.'

Quite naturally, Mary at first thought that she hadn't heard her son correctly and just carried on with her fruitless search. But then her son spoke again, and this time there was no mistaking what he'd said.

'Nan came last night and told me she wanted the medal. She said she liked it and wanted to keep it with her. Then she said I wasn't to be upset, because I would get it back one day.'

The medal was never seen again. Mary's rational mind told her that there must be a simple explanation. She told herself that her son must have been dreaming, and that the medal really was just lost somewhere in the house. She even considered the possibility that her son had lost the medal and had merely invented the story about the dream as an excuse. It was a possibility that she rejected instantaneously, for she just knew instinctively that he was telling the truth. Mary was desperate for a rational explanation, but just couldn't find one.

Did Mary's mother return from the grave to retrieve her precious medal? I don't think so, although I appreciate why people might be drawn to such a conclusion for a number of reasons. However, neither do I believe that the medal was simply mislaid. Spiritual forces were at work here, but readers will have to make up their own mind as to just what kind.

22

Merpeople

Very few people actually believe in mermaids – or mermen, come to that. In a way this is perfectly understandable, for the whole concept of creatures which are half-fish and half-human sounds completely bizarre. From a purely logical standpoint, though, there's nothing that really works against the notion that they may indeed exist.

Let's look at the facts. If you believe in the theory of evolution, there's no reason why a proto-human creature couldn't have veered off the evolutionary tree millions of years ago and developed into an aquatic version of ourselves. We supposedly evolved out of the oceans, so why couldn't some creatures evolve back into them? Look at all the fantastic variations of life on earth, all of which, according to evolutionists, sprung from the same source! But what if you don't believe in evolution? What if you believe that all life was directly created by God? There's still no reason to disbelieve in mermaids and mermen, for an all-powerful deity can create whatever it wishes.

Now all of this is a bit philosophical, I admit, and as this isn't meant to be a philosophical book I don't want to go too deeply into the pros and cons of whether or not merpeople exist. I simply wish to record that it isn't entirely impossible. How could we know? There are hundreds, if not thousands, of aquatic creatures still awaiting discovery, so if mermen and mermaids did exist they could be inhabiting parts of the ocean hitherto unexplored. The only way we'd know, of course, is if we could actually see one. Intriguingly, many people claim to have done just that.

In *The Times* newspaper of 8th September 1809, a Scottish schoolmaster named William Munro wrote that he had encountered a mermaid whilst walking along the coast at Sandside Bay. According to Munro the creature had flowing brown hair, ruddy cheeks, blue eyes and a mouth 'of natural form'. She had perfectly normal 'breasts, abdomen, arms and fingers' too, and was actually combing her hair. After approximately four minutes she plopped back into the sea and was never seen again, at least by the good headmaster. Scotland has had more than its fair share of mermaid sightings, but they don't stop at the border. They've been seen off the Northumbrian coast, too.

A mermaid was allegedly spotted by two schoolboys off the shore at Newbiggin-by-the-Sea in the 1920s, and although they were scolded by their parents for 'making up stories', both resolutely stuck to their guns and insisted they'd seen a woman with a fish-tail jumping in and out of the briny. My only source for this was an undated cutting from an unidentifiable old magazine given to me by fellow researcher Allan Tedder, but I have no reason to doubt its veracity.

A similar incident took place back in September 1962, when two men travelled from Beadnell to the coast and boarded a boat. They then set off on a fishing trip which took them to Staple Island, a little further north up the coast. They briefly glimpsed a mermaid-like creature whose upper torso was above the waterline. They did not, in fact, realise that the woman was a mermaid at all until she 'flipped over' and for a split second they saw her tail.

Is there a rational explanation for mermaid sightings that doesn't actually involve believing in them? Some say there is. In fact, there are two aquatic mammals which, surprising though it may seem, have often been mistaken for humans. The manatee and the dugong look nothing like humans close-up, but from a distance they really can be misleading.

The problem is that many witnesses have claimed to see merpeople really close up, and have described things like skin texture, hair colour and even eye colour. It's difficult to see how they could have mistaken a manatee or a dugong under such circumstances.

Whatever merpeople are, I really don't think we can afford to be arrogant and deny their existence.

23

Pixie-Led

The ancient, pre-Christian beliefs of the old kingdom of Northumbria do not die easily. Many of them, although not immediately visible, hover just underneath the surface of the region's culture. Belief in elemental spirits, such as elves, gnomes, fairies and dwarves has still not disappeared completely. Most people treat such beliefs with scorn, it is true, but more than a few take them quite seriously – particularly in the more rural areas. Many Northumbrians still believe that pixies may also exist.

Pixies are said to be capricious creatures: nice to humans one day, vindictive towards them the next. 'You never know quite how you're on with them you know', said one Rothbury pensioner I interviewed. 'The last time I saw one was in the late 1980s. I was walking to the shop to get my paper one morning and it just popped out of an alleyway and ran across the road.'

I asked the man exactly what the creature had looked like.

'Small, pointy-eared and suited in green', he replied.

And how had he known it was a pixie he'd seen, and not some other sort of 'elemental'?

'Because *all* pixies look like that', he retorted brusquely.

Pixies may seem cute the way they're portrayed on children's TV, but according to legend they aren't to be messed with. Pixies, it is said, can lure you into their world; an alternate dimension where time travels much faster. In fact, time is said to pass *seven times* faster than here on earth. You may spend a week in the abode of the pixies, but when you return to our world – if you're lucky enough to get back to our world at all, that is – nearly two months will have gone by.

Some elemental creatures in Northumbrian folklore protect themselves in the same way that animals (and sometimes humans) do; with physical violence. Pixies are not beyond this; however, as a rule, they prefer to mess with our minds as opposed to our bodies. This, in folklore and within the field of paranormal research, is usually referred to as being 'pixie-led'.

There's an old belief in Northumbrian folklore that if you should accidentally stray into the territory of 'the little people' without invitation, you will be pixie-led to prevent you seeing things they don't want you to. In this case, being pixie-led literally means being led around in circles. I know of people who've been pixie-led in this way, and have tried to approach their motor car which is merely yards away in front of them. They will carry on walking, but never get any nearer to the vehicle. Of course, many would not only deny the existence of pixies, but would also go as far as to say that even if they did exist, the idea of them being able to confuse people in this way is nonsense. However, quantum physics has taught us that our conception of 'reality' is really an illusion and that the world is far stranger than we might have hitherto imagined. Pixies, if they exist, may possess natural abilities which enable them to manipulate or distort time and space in ways that we humans can scarcely comprehend. If physical principles such as time, space, matter, force and motion can become distorted, anyone subjected to them could experience some very weird phenomena indeed.

Of course, it could well be that some people who have seemingly been pixie-led may in reality be suffering from some illness or other condition which caused these sensations. However, this certainly can't explain away all cases. Take that of George Hall who was pixie-led at Berwick-upon-Tweed in 2007. George had visited Berwick for the day on business and decided to lunch at a local pub. The pub was approximately ¾ mile from where he'd had his appointment, and so he set off to walk there instead of driving.

'The first thing I noticed', said George, 'was that I became hot and clammy. I don't normally perspire much, but beads of sweat were running down my face. I kept walking in what I was sure was the right direction but I couldn't find the pub at all. I realised at one point that I'd passed a particular landmark twice, and couldn't understand how I'd gone around in a circle, as I know Berwick quite well. When I passed it for the third time, I started to panic and thought there was something wrong with me.

'I stopped for a moment to catch my breath and decided to go back to my client's shop. I remember walking across a car park and found myself standing outside a big, white house. I took my jacket off because by now I was so hot I thought I'd pass out. Everything seemed to be just a blur, but eventually I made it back. I don't know what came over me as I'd never had an experience like that before.'

What intrigued me about George's account was the fact that it was only after he took off his jacket that he seemed to regain his senses. There is an old folk remedy which allegedly 'cures' a person who is pixie-led. When one suspects that the pixies have been at work, it is said that one should immediately take one's coat or jacket off, turn it inside out and put it back on. This, it is said, confuses the pixies and breaks their spell over their victim. Sceptics will pour scorn on this, but I know people who claim to have tried it and they swear it works.

Was George really pixie-led that day, or simply suffering from heatstroke? Did the removal of his jacket really confuse the pixies, or simply help lower his body temperature and therefore allow him to think more clearly? We may never know. However, I've no doubt that the experience of being pixie-led, whatever its cause, is a real one.

24

Sea Monsters

Of all the cryptozoological animals that are believed to grace our planet – Bigfoot, Yeti, the Loch Ness Monster and all – it seems to me that the most likely to exist are sea monsters; as yet taxonomically unclassified creatures that inhabit the remote depths of our oceans.

Sea monsters have a long historical pedigree stretching back to the dawn of human history. However, I'd venture that no part of our globe has a richer history when it comes to leviathans than Scandinavia and the area of the North Sea; cold, dark and tempestuous, the very atmosphere breeds images of sea monsters in our heads whether they really exist or not.

But I truly believe they do. There was a time, aeons ago, when gigantic creatures thrived in our oceans like fish. Conventional wisdom suggests that they are all extinct now, but we simply can't be dogmatic about that. It's almost a cliché now to say that we know more about the surface of the moon than we do about the beds of our oceans. Sea monsters may be the stuff of legends, but legends can be true.

The most common type of monster – for want of a better word – seen off the Northumbrian coast has been the plesiosaur-like, long-necked beast which looks like Nessie, the difference being not so much its appearance but the fact that it lives in a saltwater environment as opposed to a freshwater one.

Tales of such a creature go back to the 11th century when the bodies of mutilated people began to appear on the beaches of Holy

Island and the Northumbrian coast with disquieting frequency. This went on for about three hundred years or so. Some tried to put the mutilations down to crabs, eels and other predators which, allegedly, had damaged the corpses before the sea deposited them on dry land. This isn't impossible, but it seems curious to me that the same injuries – the removal of the eyes, hands and feet – were so consistent. It is also hard to understand why, if such a natural process was at work involving crustaceans and eels, the phenomenon only lasted for three centuries or so and has now all but ended. Many thought the monster – commonly called the Shony – was to blame.

One of the most inspiring sightings I've came across took place in the year 1881. The details are sparse – I'm not sure exactly where the event occurred, or in what month, except that it was off the coast of Northumbria, and seemingly involved a Scottish fishing vessel called the *Bertie*. The *Bertie*, which had sailed south from its Scottish port, was out in the North Sea during reasonably calm conditions.

During the afternoon of the day in question, whilst the crew was going about its business, the relatively still surface of the 'German Sea' (as it was then called) was disturbed by the head and neck of a large sea creature breaking through the waves. Startled, the captain alerted the rest of the crew who all came running to see the 'monster'. They were not to be disappointed. They became very concerned indeed, however, when the creature proceeded to attack the boat. It repeatedly banged its tail against the hull, and also occasionally its head. So worried was the captain that his vessel would be damaged, he instructed a crewman to fetch his rifle from his cabin. As soon as the man returned, the captain ordered him to fire at the creature. He did so and the creature desisted from its attacks before sinking beneath the surface, but only for a while. Just when the crew thought they'd gained the better of the situation, it returned and renewed its attack upon the vessel with much more vigour and venom than before.

For several hours the captain attempted to sail away from the creature, to put a healthy distance between the boat and its attacker. Nothing seemed to work and, as dusk settled in, the sailors were convinced that it was only a matter of time before the hull would be compromised and both they and the boat they were sailing in would perish.

They must have been grateful, then, when for no apparent reason the monster suddenly stopped its attacks and dove beneath the waves. An eerie calmness overtook the boat as the captain ordered his men to sail straight for home with their story.

If the crew members of the *Bertie* are to be believed, the same creature that was blamed for killing and mutilating people several centuries earlier – or one of its descendants, at least – may still have been making a nuisance of itself in the 19th century.

There is more substantial evidence that the Shony was also around in the middle of the 20th century.

On Thursday, 9th November 1986, a columnist for *The Shields Gazette* recounted a fascinating tale of a Shony encounter which had taken place forty years earlier. The sighting wasn't in Northumberland strictly speaking, but only a short trip southwards to Tyneside – close enough to make a working hypothesis that the same kind of creature could be involved.

In the year 1946, the wreck of a ship called the *Eugenia Chandris* was lying on the bottom of the North Sea, just off the coast of South Shields. Salvage work was taking place, and at the business end of the operation was a steamer called the *Black Eagle*. At some point a crew member of the steamer saw something very strange indeed in the water –a large 'head and neck' pointing skyward to the approximate height of six feet.

All credit to this sailor and the rest of the crew; they weren't fazed at all by the appearance of the creature. Both fascinated and excited, they actually decided to give chase. Now the *Black Eagle* was equipped with four motorboats, and it dawned upon the crew that the best way of getting a better look at the monster was to use one of these in the chase. Several crew members – the account doesn't detail exactly how many – quickly set off on what must surely have been the strangest task of their careers.

As they drew close to the creature, which had essentially remained perfectly still up till this point, it suddenly seemed to react to the presence of the boat. It turned and swam southwards to the end of Marsden Bay, its head and neck still visible above the waterline, although not quite as much. The sailors simply speeded up in pursuit.

When the creature reached the far end of the bay, it suddenly stopped and sank beneath the waves. The boat reached the same spot merely seconds later, but the crew could see nothing. Then, to their amazement, the monster suddenly reared up out of the water behind them and started heading back north towards the *Black Eagle*. Once again, the sailors in the motor boat set off in hot persuit. However, to their frustration, the creature once again sank beneath the waves out of sight. The boat circled the spot, each sailor peering into the water to see if there was any sign of the leviathan. There wasn't – not until it popped out of the water again behind them and sped off to the south. This cat-and-mouse game went on for approximately ten minutes, and it is patently obvious that the creature was toying with them. Back and forth the monster and its trackers went along the bay, until the creature seemingly tired of the pastime and eventually sank beneath the waves for good.

The monster still puts in an appearance from time to time, but all attempts to identify it have failed.

25

Changelings

No one who reads the news regularly can be unaware of the horrible phenomenon of child abduction. When any child is taken from its parents, it naturally causes outrage and an outpouring of sympathy for the parents. However, when the child is a newborn baby, it seems to galvanise that collective outrage even more.

Why do people steal babies? Some women, particularly those who have lost a child or cannot give birth to one naturally due to illness or disability, eventually become desperate to become a mother. Sometimes, this desire consumes them and becomes an obsession. They will stoop to doing the unthinkable, stealing someone else's child and passing it off as their own. Others, engaged in the ruthless 'child marketing' underworld, will actually steal babies and then attempt to sell them on the black market. Outrageous as these occurrences are, such events are inevitably seen as the work of deranged or criminally-minded human beings. However, it isn't that long ago that 'elemental' creatures such as fairies and elves were also believed to steal human children. The twist was that they wouldn't simply steal a human child, but would actually replace it with one of their own. Fairy and elfin babies are said to be almost indistinguishable from human ones, and it is only as they grow that the presumed 'parents' will notice odd physical characteristics: large, almond-shaped eyes, pointed ears, extremely long fingers and large feet, to mention but a few.

Bizarre though these accounts may seem, there may be a perfectly rational explanation for them. There is a disease called Marfan syndrome which can produce in sufferers many of the physical characteristics associated with elves. It is believed that some of the Egyptian pharaohs and their families suffered from this genetic defect. Now in ages past Marfan syndrome wasn't recognised as a disease, so one can understand how parents of Marfan syndrome children would naturally assume their child must have been swapped at birth for an elven baby. After all, with every passing day they were looking more and more *like* an elf.

Northumberland was the heartland of both elfin and fairy kingdoms. Hence, tales of such baby-swaps were repeated with disturbing frequency. When an elfin and a human child were surreptitiously exchanged, both were known as changelings. The question is, why would elves or fairies want to exchange one of their own offspring for a human one?

Theories abound. Some believed that fairies placed great emphasis on physical beauty, so if they gave birth to an ugly baby they would swap it for a better-looking human one. To others, the motives were believed to be both military and political. Human babies could be stolen and reared as loyal fairy or elfin subjects. However, as they looked like normal humans they could be covertly introduced into human society without drawing attention to themselves. These 'sleepers' could then work to bring down human society from within. Intriguingly, there are similar explanations given for the activities of elemental creatures in Arabia and Asia.

Inevitably, those who were worried about their children being taken, started to devise ways of defending their homes and families from marauding elves and fairies. One trick was to place a piece of bread in the bottom of the baby's cradle. The reasoning behind this has been lost in the mists of time, but one theory is that bread, as in the Bible, represented the body of Christ, so placing bread in the cradle was tantamount to having Jesus personally present as your child's protector. Did it work? I don't really know, and there are no statistics to help us.

Then again, one could also try sprinkling salt around the cradle. Salt has the reputation of being a 'spiritual cleanser' in a number of different cultures, and there's no reason to think that Northumbrians in past times thought any differently. With some, leaving symbols of a more pointed nature, both literally and symbolically, was a preferred method. A sharp knife, a baking skewer, a sewing needle, a nail or a pin in the cot was said to be an effective remedy against the attentions of elfin or fairy baby-snatchers. But there was a very important caveat: all of these items had to be made of iron, a substance which, according to legend, produces a distinctly adverse effect on fairies and elves.

Some measures ranged from the quaint to the absolutely obscure. It was wildly believed that a working man's boot placed in the cradle also acted as a deterrent. Here, the symbolism is somewhat harder to decipher. Perhaps the boot symbolised the presence of the father himself, protecting his newborn child. It was said that the boot had to be left in the cradle for seven days.

I once met a young man who claimed to be a changeling. He was extremely tall and thin, his fingers were unusually long, his face delicately pointed at the chin. His feet were unusually large, and his ears somewhat pointed. I have to confess that he really did look like an elf. He believed that, at birth, he'd been swapped by his elfin parents who had stolen the child of his human 'parents' and left him in its place. The young man couldn't have been unaware of his unusual appearance, and this is where things get difficult to fathom. Was he really a changeling, or did he merely come to believe that he was because of the way he looked? Once again, I have to confess that I really just don't know.

It's easy to dismiss such stories as fantastical, but there is a remarkable consistency to be found in the stories of those who actually claim to have been to the elven or fairy kingdoms. Part of the problem, I think, is the 'cutsie-pie' image that many people in the West have of such creatures as elves and faeries: gossamer wings, tiaras, green, pointy hats with a bell on the top, magic wands … it's hard to incorporate such artefacts into any vignette which demands to be taken seriously. However, we need to remember that this 'cutsie-pie' image is largely one of our own making. In reality, elves, fairies, gnomes and other elementals are oft-invisible, potentially dangerous and certainly not to be sniggered at. If one finds it hard to believe in such entities, then perhaps it is our perception that needs adjusting.

People who feared that their child would be replaced by a changeling – and still do – are not simple-minded country bumpkins. They're people who have the vision to realise that there are things in this world far stranger than fiction or fantasy.

26

The Wyrm of Spindleston Heugh

About three miles west of Bamburgh Castle lies Spindleston, home of the 'Wyrm of Spindleston Heugh' – 'heugh' being an ancient colloquialism for a ridge or raised neck of land. The story survives in many forms, and the Reverend Robert Lambe, vicar of Norham – seventeen miles away – once penned the tale in verse. His literary talents have been rightly criticised, but his work is useful in that it may contain elements of the true story which are not found in other versions.

The tale centres on a royal dynasty with its seat at Bamburgh Castle itself. Although precise details are not given, certain characters are named, which enables us to determine with a fair degree of accuracy the time period during which the incident took place. The reigning Anglo-Saxon king at Bamburgh, in the setting of the story, is usually called Ida, Idda or Eda.

History testifies that there was indeed an Ida connected to Bamburgh. He was an Anglo-Saxon warlord who landed on the Yorkshire coast in the middle of the 5th century. He must have taken a great deal of satisfaction in this, for it was Ida's own grandfather, Ossa the Knifeman, who had landed there decades earlier and defeated no less a foe than the legendary British King Arthur. Ida marched north to Bamburgh without delay, and proceeded to unite the rag, tag and bobtail bands of his scattered countrymen under one flag. In this manner was the kingdom of

Bernicia born, the forerunner of the mighty Northumbrian nation. Ida died a dozen years later, so we know that the incident in question must have occurred within that twelve-year window.

Ida had twelve sons, six of whom were born to his wife and six to concubines. Due to the rather turbulent nature of the king's household, there is a degree of uncertainty over the identity of the wife who plays a central role in our story, but we need not concern ourselves too much with this. What we do know is that Ida's principal wife died, and he decided to take a replacement. For this reason he set out – probably around the year AD 550 – to find a bride.

One of the king's favourite daughters, referred to in the legend as Margaret, was left in charge of the castle during her father's absence, and did her utmost to get the castle ready for his return.

When Ida returned to Bamburgh with the new queen, the couple were greeted by the chieftains of all the Anglo-Saxon bands along the Borders. Margaret went to the fore and – trying to get off on the right foot with her new stepmother – told her that everything was now hers and that she would endeavour to make her happy in any way she could. It so happened that one of the chieftains who sat on his horse nearby overheard this. He had never seen the Princess Margaret before, and was taken both with her beautiful countenance and pleasant manners. Quite moved, he said aloud, 'This princess of the North surpasses all the female kind in beauty, and in worth'.

This kind gesture seems to have delighted Ida and his daughter, but it certainly did not please the new queen who hated anyone who stole the limelight from her. 'You may well have excepted me', she snapped at the chieftain bitterly. From that moment on, Margaret was living on borrowed time. At this point the story drifts into the realms of the fabulous, but we will relate it nonetheless.

Shortly afterwards, the queen, using witchcraft, turned young Margaret into a 'laidley [loathsome] wyrm'. Devastated, the princess slithered/crawled (or whatever) to a cave at nearby Spindleston Heugh and took up residence there.

Now one of Ida's sons, poetically known as the Childe of Wynde, was taking care of some business in Europe when word reached him that a wyrm was causing mayhem near his father's castle. As the Childe of Wynde was particularly close to his sister Margaret, he feared for her safety and made plans to travel home immediately, not realising that it was Margaret – in wyrm form – who was causing all the trouble. Instead of simply hiring a boat – nothing ever goes smoothly in dragon stories – the Childe and his men built their own ship with three masts carved out of rowan trees and silk sails. According to the aforementioned poem by the vicar of Norham, they,

> *...went on board and the wind with speed*
> *Blew them along the deep,*
> *At length they spied a large square tower*
> *On a rock so high and steep.*

The crew recognised Bamburgh Castle and hastily made for shore. Unfortunately, the evil queen saw the ship and recognised its peculiar handiwork as that of the Childe of Wynde, and assumed – wrongly – that the prince must have discovered what had happened to his sister. She then sent out three (or in some versions, two) evil companions known as the 'witch wives' to psychically/magically attack the craft and send it to the ocean floor. Their plan was foiled, however, by the fact that the masts of the ship were made from rowan wood, which protected the sailors against this dark chicanery. Not to be outdone, the queen sent out an armed gang on another boat with the sole brief of dispatching the Childe of Wynde to the hereafter. The hero of the story put them to rout and carried on regardless.

But there was further drama. Poor Margaret was slowly being consumed by the wyrm-like nature, and her real personality was fast fading away. As the boat carrying the Childe of Wynde landed,

The wyrm leaped up, the wyrm leapt down,
She plaited around the stone;
And as the ship came in to land
She banged it off again.

Frustrated but not dispirited, the Childe steered the ship away and put ashore further north at Budley Sand. Still not realising that the wyrm was in fact his sister, he tracked it down and made ready to kill it with his sword. However, just as the Childe of Wynde was about to let rip, the wyrm spoke,

Halt thy sword and bend thy bow,
And send me kisses three;
For though I am a poisonous wyrm,
No harm I'll do to thee.

After a little persuasion, the hero kissed the wyrm three times as requested and the creature promptly retired to the farthest reaches of the cave. Moments later, the metamorphosed Margaret emerged, much to the amazement of her brother. The couple then made haste for Bamburgh Castle, where King Ida was delighted to find that rumours of his daughter's demise had been greatly exaggerated.

The Childe of Wynde, however, was more preoccupied with the wicked queen. He promptly turned her into a toad – served her right, say we – and declared that she would hop around Bamburgh till doomsday.

Now parts of this tale would have done the Brothers Grimm proud and, broad-minded though I am, I would not suggest for one moment that all of the preceding story should be taken literally. However, much of the story is, paradoxically, factual. Like much else that happens within the ancient and mysterious land of Northumbria, it will forever remain a mystery.

Bibliography

Hallowell, Michael J., *Mystery Animals of Northumberland & Tyneside* (CFZ Press, 2008)

Hallowell, Michael J., *Paranormal South Tyneside* (Amberley Publishing, 2009)

Henderson, William, *Folklore of the Northern Counties of England & the Borders* (Longmans, Green & Co.,1866)

Richardson, Moses Aaron, *The Local Historian's Table Book, Vol. II* (J. R. Smith, 1845)

Richardson, Moses Aaron, *The Local Historian's Table Book, Vol. III* (J. R. Smith, 1846)

Ritson, Darren W. & Hallowell, Michael J., *Ghost Taverns of the North East* (Amberley Publishing, 2009)

Robson, Alan, *Grisly Trails and Ghostly Tales* (Virgin Books, 1992)

Underwood, Peter, *The A–Z of British Ghosts* (Chancellor Press, 1992)